CHASING THE DREAM

BANTAM BOOKS
New York   Toronto   London   Sydney   Auckland

CHASING
THE
DREAM

My Lifelong Journey
to the World Series

An Autobiography by
Joe Torre
with
Tom Verducci

CHASING THE DREAM
A Bantam Book

PUBLISHING HISTORY
Bantam hardcover edition / April 1997
Bantam mass market edition / March 1998

ISBN 0-553-57907-X

Published simultaneously in the United States and Canada

Bantam Books are published by Bantam Books, a division of Bantam
Doubleday Dell Publishing Group, Inc. Its trademark, consisting of the
words "Bantam Books" and the portrayal of a rooster, is Registered in
U.S. Patent and Trademark Office and in other countries. Marca
Registrada. Bantam Books, 1540 Broadway, New York, New York
10036.

To my wife, Ali, for renewing my faith in life, giving me inspiration to live and believe in myself, being my best friend, and encouraging me to chase my dream.

—J. T.

For Kirsten, my love and inspiration.

—T. V.

ACKNOWLEDGMENTS

Many people have helped me put this book together. I would especially like to thank Irwyn Applebaum, Bantam's publisher, whose commitment and enthusiasm for this book has been unwavering. Brian Tart, my editor, is Bantam's Derek Jeter, in that he never faltered in his "we will win" attitude. He along with his hardworking assistant, Ryan Stellabotte, made the perfect double-play combination. Chris Tomasino, my literary agent and bench coach, who is a lot easier on the eyes than Don Zimmer, was tireless in her drive for perfection. I thank Bob Rosen, without whom this project would not have gotten off the ground. Tom Verducci deserves all my appreciation for the constant calm, eloquence, and style with which he handled the madness of *Chasing the Dream*. He is my MVP.

I truly value the contributions of the following people, not only to this book, but in my life: Rae, Sister Marguerite, Frank, Ali, Matt Borzello, Bing Devine, Bob Gibson, Jack Kennedy, George Kissell, Stan London, Ed Maull, Dal Maxvill, Tim McCarver, Jim McElroy, Marvin Miller, Dale Murphy, John Parascandola, Joe Ponte, Arthur Richman, Arthur Sando, Daniel "Rusty" Staub, and Bob Uecker.

CONTENTS

CHASING THE DREAM

CHAPTER 1

Brotherhood

IN THE COOL OF A BREEZY OCTOBER Sunday afternoon, I sat next to my mother in the upper deck of Milwaukee County Stadium—between home plate and third base—as my brother Frank prepared to bat in the fourth game of the 1957 World Series against the New York Yankees. The Yankees were leading the Series two games to one. Frank was a first baseman for the Milwaukee Braves, having made it to the big leagues only the year before. I was a chubby seventeen-year-old kid, and I'd never seen anything this exciting in all my life.

I had been to World Series games before this trip to Milwaukee, but all of them had been back home in New York. I had seen my beloved New York Giants lose at the Polo Grounds to the Yankees in 1951—the last World Series for Joe DiMaggio and the first for Mickey Mantle and Willie Mays. I had been at Yankee Stadium for Game Five of the 1956 World Series, when Don Larsen of the Yankees pitched his perfect game against the Brooklyn Dodgers. And I had watched the Yankees and the Milwaukee Braves split the first two games of the 1957 World Series at Yankee Stadium. I had always looked forward to going to the ballpark to watch a World Series game in New York. But it also felt like business as usual—like another day at the office. Because of the great successes of the Yankees, Giants, and Dodgers, the World Series almost never left the boroughs of New York City in the years I was growing up. From the time I was nine years old, in 1949, to that first time the Braves brought the World Series to Milwaukee, all but four of the forty-six World Series games in that span were played in New York. The Phillies managed to host two games in Philadelphia in 1950, and the Indians hosted two games in Cleveland in 1954. Otherwise the World Series was as New York as an egg cream and Coney Island.

Only when I went to Milwaukee did I really learn just how precious and thrilling the World Series is, especially when my own brother made his first World Series start in Game Four. The town was absolutely nuts about the Braves. For Milwaukee fans it was a time as special as your first love. The ball club had moved there from Boston only four years earlier. The streets and stores of the downtown area were covered with banners and signs wishing their team good luck. Many of the signs said "Go Bushville" because some of the Yankee players, apparently not enamored of having to go to a small midwestern city, had referred to Milwaukee as "the bushes." The truth is, the Braves had outdrawn the Yankees during the season by more than 700,000 people. It was a great baseball town that called itself "Baseball's Main Street." I never had liked the Yankees—everybody in my family grew up fans of the Giants and the National League—and it really angered me that they looked down on having to go to a small town to play the World Series.

I had been to County Stadium before, to visit Frank during the 1956 regular season, but this was very different. I never had before felt this kind of electricity in the air. Before the game I was in the Braves clubhouse talking with Frank when I happened to look up and see Desi Arnaz, one of the biggest television stars of the day, standing right there next to me. I never had seen County Stadium packed like this before either. Every seat was filled. There were 45,804 people there for Game Four. Almost every one of the men wore a jacket and tie—some of them wore an overcoat and hat as well —and just about all of the women, my mother included, wore a dress and hat. My mother, who was fifty-two years old at the time, had come to Milwaukee on the first plane ride of her life. My sister Rae also sat with us. Another sister, who was born Josephine but took the name Sister Mary Marguerite when she became a nun in the Ursuline order, was in a convent and unable to make the trip.

The stadium, built for the Braves in 1953, still sparkled with newness. As Frank came to bat in the fourth inning, I could see the red, white, and blue bunting gently billowing all around the ballpark on the railing to the first row of the stands—and even on the outfield fences. I could see the spruce and fir trees, called Perini's Woods, behind the center-field fence and the Veterans Administration Hospital on Mockingbird Hill overlooking right field. The patients watched the games for free from there. And I could see the Yankees' pitcher, a right-hander named Tom Sturdivant, who had won sixteen games that year, wind up and deliver a pitch to my brother. Frank connected so solidly that I could hear the crack of the bat even in the upper deck. The baseball flew high toward right field. Frank wasn't a home run hitter. He had hit only five home runs all year, three of them with help from the cozy dimensions of the Polo Grounds. But the baseball kept carrying and carrying and carrying until it finally disappeared into a jubilant mass of people in the bleachers. My brother had just hit a World Series home run.

Everybody screamed with joy. My mom shot up out of her seat with such force that her hat flew off her head. "That's my son!" she yelled. A man sitting near us said, "You can't be his mother. Why would you be sitting up here in the upper deck?" My mom, ever the generous person, had given the better tickets we got from Frank down in the field-level boxes to some friends. I felt enormous pride as I watched my brother run around the bases. I got choked up. I couldn't wait to go back to my neighborhood in Brooklyn and talk to all those Dodgers fans about my brother and his World Series home run. Frank was a clutch player. He had proved himself under the ultimate test.

Frank's home run gave Milwaukee a 4–1 lead. The Yankees, though, tied the game with two outs in the ninth inning on a three-run home run by Elston Howard. When the ball cleared the fence, I grew sick to my stomach. I felt even worse in the tenth inning, when Hank Bauer hit a triple off Warren Spahn to knock in Tony Kubek to give the Yankees a 5–4 lead. The Yankees were three outs away from taking a three-games-to-one lead in the Series. But then Nippy Jones was hit in the foot by a pitch—reaching first base only after he showed umpire Augie Donatelli the shoe polish on the baseball. Johnny Logan doubled home the tying run. And then Eddie Mathews whacked a home run, and the place went crazy. The Braves won, 7–5.

After the game I went into the Braves clubhouse. It was the happiest time of my life. The clubhouse looked spacious and new, even though by today's standards it is considered lacking for its current tenants, the Brewers. It reminds me of the way I look at the house where I grew up in Brooklyn on Avenue T. I always thought that house was big. I look at it now—Rae still lives there—and I can't believe how small it seems.

From the dugout the Braves players walked up a concrete ramp and a small flight of steps to enter the clubhouse at a back corner. The manager's office, belonging to Fred Haney at the time, was on the immediate right. Farther into the room, on the same side as the manager's office, were the sinks and shower room. The lockers lined the perimeter of the room. The players seemed huge to me, much larger in the clubhouse than on the field. Joe Adcock, the regular first baseman who had been replaced by Frank that day because of a slump, was six foot four inches and 210 pounds. Eddie Mathews, the third baseman, was six foot one, 190 pounds, and strong as a bull. Catcher Del Crandall was six foot two and 180 pounds. Henry Aaron, the team's star twenty-three-year-old outfielder, seemed to be the only one who was slightly built, but even then I noticed how powerful his hands and wrists looked.

The players were elated. They grabbed bottles of Coca-Cola and beer out of a metal tub in the center of the room. They didn't have refrigerated dispensers then. They'd just unload the bottles from wooden boxes into a large metal tub with a drain at the bottom, then put in a big block of ice and an ice pick. Whenever a player grabbed a soda or beer, he'd put a mark next to his name on a big piece of cardboard tacked to the clubhouse wall. He was billed later according to how many marks were next to his name.

There were no postgame spreads of food in those days either. In fact, the Braves were the only team I knew of at the time to make anything available for the players to munch on. They had a bunch of crackers and a crock of cheddar cheese. It was, after all, the dairy capital of the world. Nowadays every home and visiting clubhouse serves a catered full-course meal to the players after each game.

During the Braves' postgame celebration, a fan came to the clubhouse door looking for Frank. He was holding a baseball. The fan explained that this was the baseball he had hit for the home run. Frank traded two tickets to Game Five for the baseball. Later Frank had every one of his teammates sign the ball. When he brought it home to Brooklyn, Rae preserved the cherished family heirloom with a coat of her clear nail polish.

I spent just about all my time in that exuberant clubhouse trying to be as inconspicuous as possible. I was a timid kid, and I kept my mouth shut, hanging close to Frank's locker. My eyes were wide open, though. I'll never forget how I felt in that Braves clubhouse after a World Series win. I knew right then it was the only place I ever wanted to be. I was lucky enough to get a peek behind the thick velvet curtain—to go backstage at the World Series—and it inspired me. That's when the World Series became my dream. I fell asleep that night dreaming about it.

I was a decent sandlot player at the time, but I knew I had many, many miles to travel to get from where I was playing to where Frank was playing. Dreaming about getting to the World Series was the same as dreaming about becoming president of the United States. It seemed so far away. You had to be blessed enough and lucky enough to get there. But I was having a hell of a good time living my dream through my brother.

Early the next morning my mother appeared on the *Today* show. Frank accompanied her on the trip to a Milwaukee TV studio. My mother was so nervous that, when they asked her who her favorite ballplayer was, she didn't say Frank. She said Gil Hodges of the Brooklyn Dodgers.

The Braves won again that day, 1–0, behind Lew Burdette's pitching. The Series then returned to Yankee Stadium for Game Six. We had better seats there, the box seats behind home plate. Yankee Stadium was a museum to me—a museum of baseball. When I walked in, I thought about all the great teams and athletes who had played there. A couple of years ago I played a round of golf at Augusta. I had the same feeling walking that course: like I was in a golf museum. The surroundings and the knowledge of all the people who had walked there before me were humbling.

In the fifth inning, with the Braves losing 2–0, Frank tagged a pitch from Bob Turley. Hank Bauer, the Yankee right fielder, drifted back to the three-foot outfield wall, near the 344 feet sign. He put one hand on the wall, stood on one leg, and reached for the ball with his glove. But the baseball sailed well over him and into the bleachers. Frank had hit another home run. This time I felt like running all the way home to Avenue T right then and there to tell my friends about it.

The Yankees won that sixth game 3–2, bringing the 1957 World Series to a seventh game. Warren Spahn was supposed to start that final game, but he was sidelined by the flu. So Haney gave the ball to Burdette, asking him to pitch on only two days of rest. I knew Burdette was tough. While shutting out the Yankees in Game Five, he took a wicked line drive off his chest. I was in the clubhouse after that game, and I saw on his chest the imprint of commissioner Ford Frick's autograph, which was on the World Series baseballs. Burdette pitched one of the greatest games in World Series history, shutting out the Yankees 5–0 in the deciding game.

My brother was a world champion—and he had the ring to prove it. It was one of the most beautiful things I had ever seen. It was a heavy gold ring with four rubies on top in the shape of a baseball diamond, with a large diamond stone in the middle. Around the rubies, inscribed in a square, it said "Milwaukee Braves. World Champions." On one side of the ring it said "1957," above the Braves' Indian logo. On the other side it said "Frank Torre. 1B." Frank wore it proudly every day.

Amazingly, Frank and the Braves made it back to the World Series against the Yankees again in 1958. Milwaukee took a three-games-to-one lead in the Series. The Braves' wives were so confident of victory, they started talking about how to spend the World Series winners' shares. One of them, Darlene McMahon, the wife of pitcher Don McMahon, bought a fur coat in New York in anticipation of the $8,000 winners' paycheck. After the Yankees won Game Five 7–0, Don didn't talk to her all the way back to Milwaukee. He knew the Series wasn't over. Sure enough, the Yankees won the last two games in Milwaukee to win the world championship.

Frank, a hero in the 1957 World Series, committed two errors at first base in the 6–2 loss in Game Seven. I waited for Frank in the clubhouse after that game. He barely spoke as we drove back to his apartment. He was so angry at himself that he was speeding through Wisconsin Avenue in downtown Milwaukee at about sixty miles per hour. A policeman stopped the car. When he walked up to the driver's window and saw who it was, the officer said, "Just take it easy, Frank, okay?" and let us go. I thought that was real nice. Frank's day was bad enough already.

Every player, manager, coach, trainer, and executive who gets to the World Series gets a ring. The winners' rings say "World Champions" and the losers' rings say "League Champions." I've seen enough other people wearing them to know that they are more elaborate these days than when Frank played. Many of the recent ones feature words or a phrase that embodies the team's season. The Atlanta Braves' 1995 world championship ring, for instance, is inscribed "Team of the '90s." Frank's 1958 World Series ring had smaller stones than the 1957 ring. It had an oval face rather than a rectangular one and it too featured the Braves' Indian logo. It was inscribed "Milwaukee Braves. National League Champions." Frank decided to turn his 1958 ring into a pendant for our mother. A jeweler removed the sides of the ring and used only the top. My mom, though, never wore jewelry, and it sat in her dresser for a while. After a couple of months I asked her if I could have it. She said sure. I brought it to a jeweler and had it turned back into a ring.

I wore that ring for several years, including during the early part of my playing career in the big leagues. My teammates and other people would see this big World Series ring and ask, "Where'd you get that?" and "What team did you play on to get that?" I got tired of having to explain that I didn't earn it, my brother did. So finally I just put the ring in a small jewelry travel pouch and left it there. Then one day in 1972 I reached into the pouch for a pair of cufflinks and noticed that the ring was gone. I figured out that while I had been at a New York hotel three or four days before that—I was there for the players' ratifications vote concluding the 1972 players' strike—someone had stolen the ring. It must have been an inside job, because nothing else in the room was disturbed.

The thief must have known we were out of the rooms at 1:00 P.M. taking the vote.

Ever since I lost the ring, Frank would tell me, "You've got to replace that ring." And then when his son, Frankie, was born in 1976, he would say, "I want you to get a ring and give it to my son." That was his way of telling me that eventually my dream would come true—that I was going to get to the World Series. Though I doubted it many times, my brother was right. At 10:56 on the night of October 26, 1996, I rushed out from the dugout onto the field at Yankee Stadium a World Series champion. Thirty-nine years after I had watched Frank hit those two World Series home runs, the same two clubs, the Braves and Yankees, had staged another grueling, unforgettable Fall Classic. This time, as manager of the Yankees, I was a part of the celebration.

As I took my team on a victory lap around Yankee Stadium, I thought, This is what I waited for my whole life. It felt even better than I ever imagined. It had taken me until I was fifty-six years old. It had taken me 4,272 major league games as a player and manager—no one had ever waited longer to get to the World Series. It had taken getting traded twice and getting fired three times. Both my parents had died years before they could have seen me celebrate the victory. And in the end it had taken the most emotional twelve months of my life: the birth of my daughter Andrea Rae; the shocking death of my brother Rocco; and a life-saving heart transplant for Frank on the eve of the clinching game of the World Series. I never expected that chasing the dream would bring me to so many magical moments, or that the road to get there would be so long and so often painful.

CHAPTER 2
Our House

RAE WAS WIELDING A KITCHEN knife when my father reached for the gun. I was nine or ten years old at the time, standing between the two of them, and scared as hell about what might happen. My father, Joe, was a New York City detective with a mean streak he never hesitated to show around the house. Lord knows my mother felt the sting of his hand more than once. She was there, too, that day at our brick row house on Avenue T in East Flatbush, Brooklyn. My father was raging at Rae, threatening her and yelling at her to put down the knife. She wouldn't put it down. So my father turned and began to reach into a dining-room drawer. I knew that was where he kept his revolver.

I didn't know what he planned to do. I didn't know what he was capable of, though I was so terrified of the man, it was easy for me to imagine the worst. Either way, I didn't want to find out. I couldn't let this madness play out any further. I grabbed the knife out of Rae's hand and put it on the dining-room table. "Here!" I said to him. And with that the confrontation ended and a calm fell over the house somehow. I don't recall what had provoked that fight, and it hardly matters because such confrontations were all too common. As long as my father was under our roof, those interludes of calm were charged with tension and anxiety, the same way that storm clouds building with rain and thunder inevitably burst forth.

Growing up, I was a nervous, self-conscious kid with hardly an ounce of confidence. I was the baby of the family, the youngest of five children, all of whom were at least eight years older than me. My shyness occurred partly because I was a fat kid. But I know I was skittish because of the threat my father represented to me as well. I know he used to hit my mother, even if I can't recall if I was present when he did. To this day I can see him raising the back of his hand to her, and then . . . I see nothing. Maybe I've just blacked out the rest in my mind. He never hit me. But sometimes that's worse than actually getting hit, especially for a child. I was always thinking, What is he going to do to me?

My father used to come home at two or three in the morning after work. I'd hear him come in, and just his presence in the house would be enough to make me nervous. He would sleep until the early afternoon. On weekends and days when there was no school, I walked around the house on eggshells, trying not to wake him. If I did make too much noise, he would pound the wall next to his bed three times slowly: Boom! Boom! Boom! That was his warning signal from his upstairs bedroom.

He usually would leave the house around four or five in the afternoon. The first thing I did when I came home from school was check to see if his car was parked outside our house. If I saw the black Studebaker out front, there was no way I was going home. I'd go to a friend's house or stay outside and play.

I remember one time—I couldn't have been more than five or six—when my parents had some friends over. I was in the upstairs bathroom urinating, except that I didn't close the door, and the acoustics were such that the sound carried extremely well. My father was so embarrassed, he flew into a rage, yelling so viciously at me in front of everyone that even my older brother Frank was afraid for me. That was pretty typical. Although he never physically hurt me, he verbally abused me often.

That's what it was like at the Torre house, at least when my father was around. Don't get me wrong—our home was filled with plenty of love too. In fact, I was smothered with attention and affection because I was so much younger than my siblings. I'll admit it—I was spoiled. Sister Marguerite thinks that my mother doted on all of us, especially me, because she lived with such pain and unhappiness in her marriage. I think she's right. I think the nervousness that pervaded our house made us cling to one another a little more tightly. Of course, my mother was especially protective of me in that environment because I was the youngest. This much I know for sure: I was loved very much, but my father frightened me.

I was born Joseph Paul Torre on July 18, 1940, in Madison Park Hospital in Brooklyn, the first in our family to be delivered in a hospital. My mother had my four brothers and sisters in the bedroom of an apartment in the Greenpoint section of Brooklyn, where my family had lived before I was born. My mother was a strong, stubborn woman who didn't like doctors. Six years earlier she had given birth to a baby girl who died almost immediately from complications, but only after she was baptized and named Theresa. Doctors advised my mother not to have any more children. I guess I was the mistake, the one who wasn't supposed to be here. I know from stories Frank told me that my father was angry when he found out my mother was pregnant with me. She was thirty-five years old.

From the moment I came home from the hospital, my mother and sisters devoted themselves to making sure I was happy. Rae, who was fourteen when I was born, and Sister Marguerite, who was ten, used to sit around and wait for me to cry, then pounce immediately with love and hugs to soothe me. Frank was the next youngest to me—although he was eight and a half when I came along. Rocco was twelve. At the end of our block, no more than a hundred yards from our house, was Marine Park. Rocco would be rushing out of the house to go play baseball there with his friends from the neighborhood, and my mother would say, "If you want to play, you have to bring Joey along." Rocco and his friends would have to push me in the baby carriage to the park. So you see, I grew up around baseball from a very early age.

My mother was born Margaret Rofrano in Italy in 1905 and came to this country as an infant. I remember asking her about our heritage, "What are we? Neapolitan? Sicilian?" She said, "You're American." That was a time when you were embarrassed about being "from the other side," especially during the war years. One memory stands out about being a kid in wartime. We used to have mandated blackouts at night in Brooklyn, where every house would have to cut its lights and draw the shades, in case the enemy was looking for land during an invasion from sea. In those days we worried that at any moment the war could spread to our shores. My brothers, sisters, and I would huddle in a tiny nook—it was no bigger than a small closet—outside our first-floor bathroom. Being the nervous kid that I was, I was petrified of the darkness and what might be out there, so sometimes Sister Marguerite would allow me the tiny concession of lighting a small votive candle in that nook.

My mom lavished her children with love and attention. At Christmastime she used to make sure we had the best presents. We would go to my grandmother Torre's house on Christmas Eve. She lived in my family's old apartment house in Greenpoint on Lorimer Street. It would always take my sisters longer than me to get in the car, for what are now obvious reasons. Before they left the house, they would throw the presents under the tree so that when we came back home later that night, it would look like Santa Claus had already made his drop. I remember one Christmas getting a Howdy Doody doll, which was *the* toy to have at the time. That was my mom—nothing was too good for us, especially me. When I attended elementary school—it was about a one-mile walk from our house—I used to come home for lunch. All the other kids were at school eating sandwiches out of brown bags. My mother would cook me eggs and a hamburger patty. I had home-cooked hot meals for lunch every day. Other times I'd come in from playing outside, and my mom would have a fresh fruit salad waiting for me in a bowl. I must have been an adult by the time I knew cantaloupe actually comes with a skin on it.

In a lot of ways my mother was a typical Italian mother. She was a fabulous and prodigious cook (my early physique was a walking, irrefutable testament to that talent) and a devout Catholic who always put her family first. She could also be very tough, although I only remember her hitting me once. I know, however, that the thought occurred to her often. Whenever she did raise her hand to strike me, she would stop herself by biting her index finger. That was my cue to get out of her reach. In those days such parenting methods weren't so unusual, at least from what I knew in Brooklyn. But mostly my mother was a loving, stabilizing influence, who always was there for me. She worked some as well. She used to earn money crocheting clothes, especially for infants. She'd sit in front of the television set and do her work. And she loved to play casino with us. You could always tell when she had good cards and was going to make a big hit on you because she would straighten them perfectly in her hands, as if proudly dressing up her children to go out on Sunday.

Sister Marguerite often said to Mom, "Oh, Frank is your favorite." And Frank used to think I was her favorite. But my mother used to have a saying whenever anybody thought she had a favorite. She'd hold up her hand with her palm open and say, "See these fingers? Cut off any of them, and it hurts just the same." Five fingers for five children. The 1996 World Series made me think of another one of her favorite lines. She always used to tell me, "Don't worry, Joe. Good things come to those who wait." And she was right about that.

Sister Marguerite says she doesn't know how my mother endured my father for so long. I think she stuck it out because she didn't want me to be harassed or embarrassed by the other kids in grammar school. Divorce was not as convenient in those days as it is now, especially for someone as religious as my mother. She went to mass every day at Good Shepherd Church, always walking through Marine Park to get there. Of course, I was really too young at that time to understand how bad things were between my parents.

My father, an Italian-American who was born in New York, actually was a very shrewd, brilliant man with a charismatic side. His mother once gave him the money needed to apply to the police academy. My father kept the money but never went. He did, though, show up for the police exam and passed it anyway. He rose quickly through the department with the kind of sharp mind and gruff manner that earned him the nickname Joe the Boss. That's what his friends would call him off duty, too, while he engaged in his two favorite pastimes: playing the horses and playing cards. He was never really a drinker. I'm not sure what caused his rage, but I know it wasn't a drinking problem.

My dad always had his ways of making people feel obligated to him. He used to carry around Italian candy, nuts, little miniature bottles of cognac, and stuff like that in boxes in the trunk of his car. He'd always be dropping off gifts to people, but not always to spread joy; he didn't mind knowing that his gift-giving would make others feel indebted to him. At Christmastime he would wrap these small gifts in packages, write little notes with them, and send them out to hundreds of people. I mean hundreds of people. He was very meticulous about it. He anticipated that some might do favors for him in return.

I used to look forward to the month or two after Christmas, when my father would be in Florida for his winter getaway. That was great for me because the house was calm without him. I didn't find out until much later that he would make these trips to Florida with a woman, whom he would eventually marry after he and my mother were divorced. I later met her and found her to be a nice woman. Unfortunately, my father abused her too. I wasn't observant enough as a child to notice that after my father spent two months in Florida he never came home with a tan. He was always playing cards. He'd go to a golf course and play cards all day with his friends.

Frank was never afraid of my father, even if he did catch his share of beatings. Frank was a street-tough kid who never took any money from him because he didn't want to feel indebted to him. When Frank was older, my father tried to use his car as leverage against him, always threatening Frank by saying he wouldn't let him use it for one reason or another. Finally one day Frank threw the keys at him and said, "Keep it. I don't want your car." By then Frank had grown to be a pretty big kid, and my father would never mess with Mom as long as Frank was in the house.

I don't think Sister Marguerite was afraid of my father either. Actually, he was rather affectionate toward her. She happened to be terribly sick with pneumonia when she was two years old. My parents thought she was going to die. My father later told her that he made all kinds of promises to Saint Theresa, his favorite saint, if only his daughter would live. Because of that episode my father treated her very well, although she grew up to resent him because of how he treated the rest of us. Now she says she's amazed that Rocco, Frank, and I grew up to be decent fathers at all, with that kind of role model. She used to use the expression "My father has loused up three lives," referring to my two brothers and me, because for a while I was irresponsible and immature. But I was lucky enough to have Rocco and Frank, both of whom were considerably older than me, as strong male figures in my life. I grew up in my teenage years with Rocco as a beat policeman and a solid family man and Frank as a professional ballplayer: two strong men in uniform. I was very proud of them and gained a respect for authority and our family name because of them. I never wanted to embarrass them by any of my actions. I drew strength, love, and friendship from Rocco and Frank—a lot more than from my father.

Rocco probably was the best ballplayer among the three of us brothers. He was a right-handed power pitcher whom the Brooklyn Dodgers wanted to sign. My father, though, refused to grant the parental permission required for any prospect under the age of twenty-one. He insisted Rocco go to college—he wanted him to become a lawyer—even though Rocco didn't care for school. He was lucky to get through high school because of his poor grades. Rather than argue with my father, he joined the navy and served in World War II. After his service time he enrolled at St. John's University for a year or two, married at twenty-two, and took a job as a policeman in Brooklyn.

Rocco was a tremendous influence on me because he was such a responsible family man. He had a completely different agenda from Frank. Frank was single through his baseball-playing days, and he was the one who always liked the action. He'd go to the horses during the daytime and the trotters at night. He loved to play cards. He had no responsibilities. Plus, my relationship with Frank was more of a professional one right up until a couple of years ago, when he became sick. Only then were you allowed to show your emotions to him.

It was tough for me to get close to Frank because he was so critical of me all the time. Rocco was a lot easier to be around and talk to. I looked forward to occasionally eating Sunday dinner at Rocco's house in Flushing. His wife, Rose, was a great cook, and later Rocco was too. In fact, as adults Rocco and I used to trade recipes. It was a very comfortable feeling to be around Rocco and to be at his happy home. I also liked to catch up with Rocco at the moonlighting jobs he would take from his police work. He worked at a gas station for a while. And he worked a couple of nights a week at the Colonnade liquor store on West Fifty-sixth Street near

Eighth Avenue. I'll never forget that place because they filmed the movie *The Hustler* right across the street.

There's no question that Rae and my mother took the brunt of my father's boorishness and saw more of his dark side than the rest of us. Rae is an absolute sweetheart, the one who grew closest to my mother as an adult because she lived at home while working for the phone company. Rae is such a kind, generous woman that most people thought, if anyone in our house would become a nun, it would be her. She was so honest that in all those years at AT&T, and later at Nynex, she refused to take home from work so much as a pencil or pad of paper—not that I didn't try planting larcenous thoughts in her brain. I'd often ask her to bring home that kind of stuff. On the whole, though, Rae passed on her trait for unabashed honesty to me. I remember one time when I was ten, going to the movie theater to see a film that required a child to be eleven years old. The clerk asked me how old I was. I was so honest that I blurted out my real age, thereby assuring that I would be denied a seat in the theater. I walked home by myself.

Another time when I was ten, my mother had to go out somewhere, and she told Sister Marguerite to baby-sit me. Sister Marguerite, though, had an interview scheduled with the Trinitarian nuns about the possibility of joining them. She did not, however, tell my mother about that. She wasn't ready to tell her she was thinking about becoming a nun, for as religious as my mother was, she probably would not like the idea of "losing" one of her daughters. It's not as if my mother would have expected her to make such a decision either. Sister Marguerite was a typically devilish, precocious, boy-crazy young woman. So now she had to make a decision: baby-sit me or go to the interview. She decided to do both. She brought me along to the interview; then, in an attempt to ensure my secrecy about this misbehavior, she bought me an ice cream soda and took me home in a taxi, which was an extravagance for us. "Now whatever you do, don't tell Mom about this," she instructed me. Of course, when my mother came home and asked me what we did, I promptly told her the whole story. Sister Marguerite was livid, but that's me. I just can't lie, I guess.

Because Rocco, Frank, and Sister Marguerite eventually moved out of the house and because I was so young, only Rae and my mother were around to deal with my father. That's probably why Rae is the only one of the children who never came to any kind of reconciliation with him. I understand that. It must have been hell. I don't remember my dad actually striking Rae, but I know many times my sister put herself in harm's way by physically defending my mother against him. I remember all the yelling going on between the three of them, and that scared me. I guess that day when Rae picked up that knife and pointed it at my father, she had reached the breaking point.

Then one day, mercifully, the terror finally ended. It was 1951, and I was eleven years old. Sister Marguerite had left home to become a nun earlier that year. The day she left, she bought me a present.

"I was going to buy you rosary beads," she said, "but I figured I might as well give you something you'd use." And then she gave me a beautiful and rather expensive baseball glove. "Every time you use it," she instructed me, "say one Our Father."

And then she was gone, semicloistered in the convent, which meant she could have visitors but she couldn't come home. She spent many of those nights crying herself to sleep over what my father was doing to our mother and our family. Rocco was out of the house too; he was married. Frank had spent most of the year playing minor league ball in Denver, where he had received many late-night telephone calls from my distraught, weeping mother. Frank's always been a tough son of a gun, a straight shooter who's not afraid to tell it like it is. And when he returned home from Denver after his season ended, that's how he laid it out to my mother.

"Mom, I'm tired of getting these phone calls in the middle of the night a thousand miles away," Frank said. "Now, listen. He has to go. And you either make the move now—because he won't do anything with me around—or when I leave for next season, I'm never coming back. Because I can't put up with this stuff anymore."

My mother agreed. It was time for them to split up. But she couldn't bring herself to tell my father. So she, Frank, Rae, and I all gathered around the dining-room table one day and called my dad in. Frank did most of the talking. He told my father that this marriage wasn't working out for anybody. The whole family wanted him out. He wouldn't have to pay any alimony or child support or anything like that. All we wanted was for him to sign the house over to my mother. That was it. My father had bought the house brand-new, back in 1935, for $5,900. We still had a mortgage on the place. Grudgingly, my father agreed. I think, inside, he was relieved because he knew our family was not a happy one. He moved out to another part of Brooklyn. I didn't speak another word to him for six years, and neither did my siblings. The little brick row house on Avenue T became a much happier place. There would be no more storms.

It turned out that I would have two failed marriages myself. Was that my father's fault? I don't think so. I made those mistakes because I was spoiled and irresponsible, though I have three wonderful kids from those marriages: Michael, Tina, and Lauren. I love them unconditionally and always have been a part of their lives. Everybody in my family was telling me in those days not to get married. That was all I needed to hear—I'd do the opposite. I thought I could do anything I wanted. I look back, and I really hate myself for the way I was. Totally spoiled. I'm sure I hurt my mother deeply with my first two marriages. In both cases I married outside the Church, without anyone from my family in attendance. I wish she had lived long enough to have known Ali, my present wife, and been there the day we walked down the aisle of the Lady Chapel behind the main altar at St. Patrick's Cathedral in Manhattan.

After my father left, I really didn't see him again until I was seventeen years old. Sad to say, he started to show up at some of my baseball games once word got out that professional scouts were looking at me. Being the kind of wheeler-dealer that he was, he wanted to be in on the action. My dad also began coming to my games because he was loosely affiliated with the Braves as a scout. In 1950 he had worked a deal with the Braves, who were based in Boston then, that he would give the club permission to sign Frank only if they gave him a scouting job. He later scouted for Baltimore. It wasn't as if we renewed our relationship right away. That happened later in the winter, when Frank was home from playing ball. Frank had the same love for card playing that my father did. And he knew that every Tuesday night my father would play gin rummy in a back room of Sirico's restaurant on Thirteenth Avenue in Bay Ridge. They'd have a dozen guys back there, smoking and gambling. They didn't play for big stakes; it was more the ritual of getting together with the guys that was important. My dad would run the whole show. Joe the Boss would scream at anybody who made a dumb move, no matter who he was.

Frank would sit in on these card games. Naturally, I always wanted to tag along with my big brother, so Frank started bringing me. He thought it was important that all of us come to some sort of peace with my father. Frank was the first of the children to begin speaking again with Dad (though it was never a full reconciliation). That was very big of him, considering he was the one who finally had had the guts to kick my father out of the house. Later on Sister Marguerite also came to an understanding with him. He would visit her at the convents, and she developed what she calls "a special love" for him. It was a love, she said, that didn't blind her to the reality of what she knew him to be: a terrible father and a dreadful husband.

With Frank's help I also developed a friendship with my father, though it was never a very close one, and I didn't see him often. I don't think he ever knew me well. I remember one time when I was in my early twenties, he gave me a leather belt as a gift. The belt was way too big for me. He had remembered me as being such a fat kid, which I no longer was.

When my mother found out that Frank and I were hanging out with my father at these card games, she was furious. Understandably, she didn't want us to have anything to do with him, and I don't believe she ever forgave him for what he did to her. Rae was the same way. I guess I managed to keep most of the feelings I had about my father repressed for many years. I just never acknowledged to myself what impact my childhood years had on me as an adult. I'd always been a very guarded person. Then during the week after Thanksgiving in 1995, only three weeks after I accepted George Steinbrenner's offer to manage the Yankees, Ali asked me to come with her to a four-day seminar on self-improvement. It was being held at a Holiday Inn in Cincinnati, her hometown. I had no idea what it was all about. I didn't know if it was about business, about life outside of baseball, or what.

"I'll go with you," I said. "I don't want you to go alone."

"Don't go just because you want to go with me," she said. "I want you to go because you want to go."

"I'll go," I insisted.

So I went. And as soon as I got there and got a sense of what it was about, I said, "Oh, shit."

Since I married Ali in 1987, I've slowly gotten a little better about expressing myself, but it hasn't been easy. Over the years she's frequently said to me, "We've got to talk." And whenever I heard that, immediately I could feel myself tense up. For some reason that was like death to me. That's why I panicked when I walked into that ballroom at the Holiday Inn and found out what was about to happen. There were about fifty people there, and they promptly broke us up into groups of six. There was one hitch: You were not allowed to sit next to your spouse or anyone else you knew. And you weren't allowed to talk with your spouse about what happened when you went home during the training. I found myself having to talk about myself and my feelings to complete strangers over the next four days. I was in agony.

On the first day I began to open up—reluctantly, but I did it. We had to stand up and answer questions like "What do you want to accomplish here?" and "What don't you like?" When it came my turn, I got up and said, "I don't like confrontation. I am uncomfortable with it." And over the course of group sessions during the next three days and nights, I gradually bared my heart and my tears to these strangers. They had ways of drawing out the emotions from everyone, including myself. You had to hold each other and look into each other's eyes. It was very emotional.

I began to understand why I never liked confrontations. I talked about my father and the way he dominated our house and abused our mother. Because of his behavior, yelling and loud noises always made me uncomfortable, and I did whatever I could to avoid those kinds of situations. As we started to dig out those kinds of things—carefully and gradually, like archaeologists—I telephoned Sister Marguerite, on the morning of the third day of the seminar, to confirm some of my findings.

"Did Dad really hit Mom?" I asked her.

"Oh, did he ever," she said. "Joey, I'm surprised

you turned out as well as you did, growing up in that house."

As we talked some more about my dad and our childhood, I started crying on the telephone. Then I rejoined my group and told them about the phone call, and I got all choked up just talking about it again. It made me feel better. I began to understand. It seems as if everybody thinks they're the only ones who have something wrong with themselves. It's like you're in a dark quiet room, thinking you're alone, but a light goes on, and you see you are surrounded by people just like you, who felt they were alone too. I get a kick out of that concept, because it helps me as a manager to understand players. I laugh, for instance, at players who want to tell you how good they are. I think what they're really trying to do is convince themselves, not you. Michael Jordan doesn't tell you how good he is. I mean, he knows he's good, and he won't back off from it. But he doesn't have to do what Dennis Rodman does, to get the attention he gets.

That weekend in Cincinnati actually helped me become a better manager. It helped my approach going into the 1996 season with the Yankees. It taught me how to relax myself by putting everything into its proper category rather than thinking I could just take on all my problems at once, which is how you get overwhelmed.

Once my father left the house in 1951, my brothers became even more important to me. Frank became especially influential because he was a professional baseball player. He had signed his first professional contract in 1950, the year I turned ten. Milwaukee Braves scout Honey Russell, the former Seton Hall University basketball coach, gave him a six-thousand-dollar bonus. Frank was such a terrific hitter in high school that he swears he never struck out, not once. He played first base and pitched. In fact, Frank pitched the Brooklyn Cadets sandlot team to a national title in 1950 at the All-American Amateur Baseball Association tournament in Johnstown, Pennsylvania. He threw a no-hitter in the final game, even though his eyes were nearly closed because of an allergy. I was in awe of my own brother.

Frank began his 1951 season in Hartford before the Braves assigned him to the Denver Bears, a Class A club in the Western League. He invited me out to Colorado to join him. I traveled from New York to Denver by train with my aunt Ella, cousin Carmela, and Rae. My life was about to change in a big way. I went to Denver as something of an average-sized ten-year-old and came home a little more than one month later an eleven-year-old blimp. I mean, I just blew up. I always had a pretty good appetite, and my mother always did a fine job attending to it. But in Denver I ate all the time.

Frank used to hang out at this place called Richard's Steak House. I can remember having my birthday party there—I had a cake as big as a desk. I used to go to the ballpark with Frank every day. But first, at about one or two in the afternoon, we'd go to Richard's for lunch. I'd devour a huge meal, usually a steak. I'd shag flies and work out at the ballpark, then eat some more during the game—maybe a hot dog or two and something else. And then after the game we'd go back to Richard's, and I'd eat another big meal—usually another slab of steak and some sort of mountainous dessert.

One thing everyone should know about Frank is that he's a world-class needler. He is always stirring the pot. And after I became this fat kid, Frank did more than needle me. He rode me mercilessly. He would call me a fat slob repeatedly, tell me what an embarrassment I was to him and the family. I hated him for this for a long time. I was a chubby kid and felt ashamed of it. One time I played a special sand-lot game at Ebbets Field in which Pee Wee Reese served as our manager. I must have made a big impression on the great Dodger shortstop. Later on Pee Wee said to Frank, "Oh, your brother likes the groceries, doesn't he?"

Another time Frank invited me back to Ebbets Field to work out with the Braves before a game against the Dodgers, playing catch and shagging flies. I must have been fifteen or sixteen. Frank, of course, had been getting all over me for years about my weight and nothing much had changed, so I guess he thought he had to enlist some help. So he told the real needlers on that Braves team—guys like Warren Spahn, Lew Burdette, and Bob Buhl—to get on my case about being so fat. He figured if I didn't believe him, maybe I'd get the message through these other guys. So when I showed up and started changing into a Braves uniform, those guys were all over me, calling me "Spaghetti Bender" and things like that. I felt so terrible that after the workout I waited until after the game started to take a shower to make sure no one would see me naked.

I really did hate Frank because he was so vicious in the way he'd get on me. I'd show him trophies that I'd won playing ball, and he'd just grumble, "Those things are worthless. They don't mean anything. You'll never be a ballplayer. You're too much a fat slob to be a ballplayer." But Frank was definitely my idol. He was doing what I wanted to do: He was a ballplayer. And that meant I had to keep jumping back in with him. I was always looking for his approval. So even though he was tough on me, the only way I was going to get that approval was to be around him and do things to make him proud of me.

But I also knew this: Frank's bark was a lot worse than his bite. He was very generous. Even when he was in the minor leagues, he'd send my mother a couple hundred dollars a month, which was big money in those days. And he'd give her a lump sum at the start of winter too. Frank would always bitch about something, but then he'd give you whatever you asked for or, usually, more than you asked for. I remember when he went off for a two-year hitch in the army during the Korean War. He actually played some ball over there while he was in Seoul. In fact, that's how he became such a good fielder; he used to take grounders on these rocky open fields in Korea. (He also volunteered for night duty over there, after a couple of nights when he awoke to discover huge rats milling around inside the tents. The rats weren't such a problem during the day, with more people walking around.) Anyway, I'd write to Frank once in a while over there. My letters to him didn't go much beyond this: "Dear Frank: Can you send me fifty bucks? Joe." Frank never failed to come through with spending money for me even from that far away. And when he came home from Korea, he paid my way through a private high school, even though all my brothers and sisters had attended public school.

There's no doubt that Frank is the most different among the Torre children. Though I'd have to say that all the brothers grew up with a chauvinistic attitude—Sister Marguerite believes that the girls in the family waited on us boys—Frank has the strongest feelings of male superiority. He's a softie inside, but he has a gruff exterior. About five years ago, before he got sick, Sister Marguerite said to him, "Do you tell your children that you love them?" And Frank looked at her like "What are you, nuts?" He said, "Why do you think I'm doing everything I do for them?" Sister Marguerite said, "But Frank, you've got to say the words." Frank had been the family's protection against our father, but he did it in the same intimidating, gruff manner my father had. He'd hate for me to say it, but I believe Frank is most like my father among the Torre boys.

Frank always had a hard edge about him. With him there's no middle of the road: people either love him or hate him. See, Frank's been a fighter his whole life. One of the best stories I know about his feistiness involves his first heart attack, right before Thanksgiving back in 1984 in Las Vegas. He'd played tennis that day with a good friend of his, Alex Failoni. He got tired a lot during the match. Several times he would have to take a break, sit down, then get up and play some more. Later, at dinner, Frank wasn't hungry and told Alex he was going back to his room. Alex thought he didn't look so great but, knowing my tough brother, said, "Ah, you'll feel better in the morning." But the more Alex thought about it, the more he grew worried. Finally, he called up Frank and said, "Let's go. I'm taking you to the doctor."

And so they jumped into a cab and went to the hospital. Frank was in pretty bad shape by then. They put him on a gurney—he was semiconscious—and he heard one doctor say, "I think we're losing him." Thankfully, they managed to stabilize him. A little while later they allowed Alex in to visit him. Frank was lying there on the table with tubes up his nose. All of a sudden, when he saw Alex, he burst out laughing.

"What the hell are you laughing about?" Alex said.

"Here I am having this massive heart attack," Frank said, "and I beat you six–love!"

There's nobody like Frank. He's always been so competitive and one of the all-time agitators, whether it's tennis, golf, or just playing gin. What he's great at is unsettling people to the point that they change their game. And he'll never give you any credit when you do something well. Whatever team I was involved in, as a kid, a pro ballplayer, or a manager, Frank would always find something to complain about. Actually, that's how I knew Frank was getting sicker in recent years. I'll never forget calling him from Hawaii before the season started in 1994, when I was managing the Cardinals. We were talking about the team, and he would just say, "Oh, that's good," and, "That sounds fine." He never argued with me. So right away I started thinking, I know he's really not feeling well. This is serious.

It's great to see Frank back to his crusty self now. He's back to agitating people, which means he's feeling a lot better. In fact, he started to feel better once we got him stabilized at Columbia-Presbyterian Medical Center in Manhattan, before the heart transplant. Sister Marguerite found that out the day we clinched the East Division. She had called me up that morning from the Nativity of the Blessed Virgin Elementary School in Queens, where she's the principal, and said, "I really can't come to the game today. I have a faculty meeting." Then she saw a picture of me on the back of *The New York*

Post. I guess I must have looked pretty bad. She said later that she saw such a sadness in my face, brought on by Frank's illness, that she called up Rae and said, "Call Joe and get tickets. We're going to the game."

We won in a rout over Milwaukee, and Sister Marguerite called Frank the next morning to tell him about what happened: the blizzard of confetti at the stadium; me coming over to the stands to give kisses to Ali, Andrea, Rae, and her; the way all of us were crying; and how we all felt Rocco's presence there with us.

"Frank," Sister Marguerite said, "I'm telling you, it was an emotional high. It was the greatest moment of my life."

Frank listened as my sister gushed on about this incredible moment. And then it was his turn.

"It was nothin'," he barked. "They've still got three rounds of playoffs to get through. That was nothin'." Leave it to Frank to snap you back to reality.

I'm forever grateful that Frank is a little rough around the edges. He was exactly what I needed, especially when our father left. I was this shy, overweight kid with terrible self-confidence who was being coddled by his mother and sisters. Frank was the kick in the butt I needed to amount to anything in life. It was Frank who toughened me up, Frank who turned me into a catcher, Frank who put me through high school, Frank who used to send me spending money even when he was off fighting in Korea, and Frank who was everything I ever wanted to be. He was a ballplayer. I may not have had a father in my life then, but I sure as hell had a hero.

CHAPTER 3

The Wonder Years

FRANK IS THE ABNER DOUBLEDAY OF paperball. Maybe no definitive proof exists that establishes him as the first person to come up with the game, but as far as I'm concerned, he was its founder. Frank always was inventing games in our neighborhood—games he passed on to me proudly, like heirlooms. One of those treasures was paperball. I'd take a brown paper bag, newspaper, or some similar paper product and roll it up into a ball. Then I'd wrap lots of rubber bands around it. The ball was nearly as hard as a rock. My buddies and I would go over to East Thirty-fourth Street, which in those days wasn't paved yet, and we'd play baseball between the houses—with specially modified rules.

The bat was a sawed-off broomstick. You had to bat on the opposite side of your natural hitting stance. The pitcher would have to lob the paperball in. If you hit the ball over a first-floor window, it was a double. Over a second-floor window was a triple. Anything on the roof was a home run. But if one of the fielders caught the ball on the fly after it hit a house, you were out. The kind of ball we used made for some interesting games. It wasn't perfectly round, so when it bounced off a house, the carom was a lot more unpredictable than one off the Green Monster in Fenway Park. Also, the ball was so hard, we did break our share of windows. The neighborhood always was alive with games like that. I lived in a neighborhood that consisted predominantly of Italian and Jewish families, with a scattering of Irish families too. It was a tight-knit neighborhood where everyone seemed to know each other and look out for each other. I hung out for years with the same group of eight to ten boys, spending much of our time playing games in the street and the park.

Frank kept us busy with his inventions, including another game in our driveway, which declined steeply from the street down to our garage. A short porch hung over the garage. Someone would throw a ball toward the top of the garage, and you'd have to jump as if you were trying to take a home run away from the other guy. Frank also showed me how to play stoopball, bouncing a rubber ball off the front steps of our house. Even though he was so much older than me, I'd play with him and his friends sometimes. I'd tag along with him as much as I could. If they happened to be one man short, I'd get to play with them. Even after Frank reached the big leagues, he'd play stickball in the street with me and my friends after the season.

The little automobile traffic we did get on Avenue T in those days knew to slow down whenever it ventured down our block. Even though the park was so close to us, we seemed always to have a punchball, slapball, touch football, stoopball, or most likely, stickball game going on in the street. A home run in stickball was a ball that traveled two sewers. When darkness came, we'd move the game closer to the streetlights and just keep on playing. Every once in a while, especially when you'd have to go fetch a foul ball out of somebody's geraniums, a cranky neighbor would bark, "Why don't you kids go play in the park?" And we'd always have a simple, logical answer: The ball doesn't bounce nearly as well in the park as it does in the street.

The Brooklyn of my youth was a place where baseball was king. Nothing compared to it. Football was a game played mostly between the twenty-yard lines with very little scoring. We would play touch football in the street and have an annual Thanksgiving Day touch football game in the park, coming home all filthy dirty and bruised for the turkey dinner. But football had yet to ignite a real interest in most people. Basketball? Sure, we played it sometimes, and I gained great fame around the neighborhood for being able to palm a basketball at an early age with my big hands. But basketball as a spectator sport was nothing. Hockey? That was another boring sport, with most games ending up 0–0 or 1–0. Of course, my friends and I played just about any kind of game, including roller hockey. I couldn't skate, so I'd always be the goalie whenever we played in the street.

Baseball was our love, plain and simple. Until Frank left to play ball himself, he and I shared a tiny bedroom upstairs in our house. The place was wall-to-wall bed, so Frank and I slept next to each other, sharing the same covers. You couldn't fit two beds in that room. I never worried about being pushed out of bed by Frank because I slept on the side against the wall. The one bookshelf in the room was filled mostly with Frank's trophies; mine were scattered around the downstairs of the house. We had one closet that barely was deep enough to accommodate hangers. We'd put ourselves to sleep talking baseball. It was a time when America's passion for the game still ran deep, but nowhere with greater fervor than in New York. We always had at least one, usually two, and sometimes three big league teams involved in heated pennant races. Most people in Brooklyn were Dodgers fans, of course, but many in the borough rooted for the Yankees, who played in the Bronx—probably because the Yankees seemed to win every year. And then there was the Torre family. We were some of the few people in Brooklyn who rooted for the Giants, who played at the Polo Grounds in upper Manhattan. For reasons that are unclear to me, my brothers and sisters were Giants fans. And so I grew up a Giants fan too. Willie Mays and Don Mueller were my favorites. I hated the Yankees because they won every year. Every once in a while I sit back and laugh that my greatest accomplishment in baseball came with a team I despised as a kid. But deep down I admired them because I knew how good they were.

Every Giants fan who grew up in New York at that time knows exactly where they were the day Bobby Thomson hit his famous home run off Ralph Branca in 1951 to win the pennant over the Dodgers. It was my happiest moment as a Giants fan. The Dodgers held a thirteen-game lead over the Giants that season as late as August 11. I found out about big leads with the Yankees: They never seem to be big enough. The Giants caught Brooklyn by finishing the season with a 37-7 run. In the last inning of the deciding game of a three-game play-off—it was 3:57 on the afternoon of October 3—Thomson hit a fastball from Branca into the left-field seats of the Polo Grounds to eliminate the Dodgers and put the Giants in the World Series. Ralph Branca's name became synonymous with being a goat while Bobby Thomson's name epitomized delivering in the clutch. I was eleven years old, talking on the telephone with Rae, who was at work, while watching the game on television. I immediately put the phone down and ran into the streets of my neighborhood, looking for any Dodgers fans I could find to gloat about my team's victory. I saw a car parked on the street, all soaped up in anticipation of a Brooklyn victory. It said "Brooklyn Dodgers. National League Champions." I got a kick out of that.

I followed baseball religiously. We were one of the first families on our block to get a television set. It must have been around 1947. I remember watching baseball games on that black and white set all the time. The New York teams would broadcast their home games. It wasn't until I left home as a ballplayer myself that I found out that not every team did that.

Despite our allegiance to the Giants, my father did take me on occasion to Ebbets Field. Though I was afraid of my father inside my house, those rare trips with him to the ballpark were great. I remember walking into this beautiful cathedral of a ballpark—and I'm amazed how the sounds of baseball there still ring clearly to me after all these years. The starting pitchers in those days would warm up right between the dugout and home plate. I can still hear the echo of the ball popping into the catcher's plump mitt as I walked up a tunnel to my seat, even before I could see the field. To a kid who was seven or eight years old, it sounded like a firecracker going off. My dad would buy me these five-by-seven pictures of the Brooklyn Dodger players that came inside white envelopes. I remember tearing open those envelopes and seeing Campanella, Hodges, Reese, Cox, Robinson, and the like.

Though I wasn't a Dodgers fan, I respected anyone who wore a big league uniform.

Later on, when my brother played for the Braves, I became a real die-hard Milwaukee fan. In fact, when the Giants bolted for San Francisco and the Dodgers took off for Los Angeles after the 1957 season, I wasn't too angry about losing my favorite boyhood team and my hometown team. I was most upset about the fact that now I would have to go to Philadelphia, which was the closest National League city, to watch Frank and the Braves play. I used to feel sick when the Braves lost. I let myself get into a situation that I sometimes do now as a manager—thinking that somehow you can influence every pitch.

One of the most painful summers I recall was 1956, when the Braves squandered their lead in the pennant race to the Dodgers. I was riveted to the radio that September, rooting for the Braves to win. The Braves had a great rivalry with the Dodgers in those years. I'll never forget being at Ebbets Field one day in 1956 when Bill Bruton of Milwaukee hit a home run off Brooklyn's Don Drysdale. Johnny Logan was the next hitter. Drysdale knocked him down with a fastball. The next time around Bruton hit another home run. This time Drysdale responded by hitting Logan with a pitch, so Logan charged the mound. Logan never reached Drysdale, but Eddie Mathews did. Mathews popped Drysdale with a punch I could see clear as day even from the stands. I can still see him throwing that punch as if it was yesterday.

Although my life revolved around baseball, I did take on some odd jobs as a teenager to earn a little money. I worked for a while as a gofer in a printing shop owned by George Russano, the father of Richie and Robbie Russano, good friends and sandlot teammates from my neighborhood. I delivered the *Brooklyn Eagle* newspaper for a short time. I also had hung out at an amusement place on Avenue S and Flatbush Avenue long enough to get some work from the owner. He'd ask me and my buddies to set up the duckpins in his bowling alley. And he had us paint the golf balls for the miniature golf; we'd dip them in buckets of paint, roll them in our hands to make sure every dimple was covered, and then place them on a bed of nails to dry. I worked briefly at the Byhoff Brothers record store on Kings Highway—not that I remember coming home with any money. I came home with albums instead. I wasn't an Elvis Presley fan. That's because all the girls liked him. I liked the rock-and-roll singers like Buddy Holly, Lloyd Price, and the Big Bopper, as well as Johnny Mathis and Bobby Darin.

Mostly, though, my brief and unproductive periods of employment served only to get in the way of my playing baseball. If I couldn't be outside playing ball, then I'd be inside playing baseball board games with my friend Johnny Parascandola, who lived around the block from me on East Thirty-fourth Street. We started out playing Ethan Allen's

All-Star Baseball—a game with spinners—and then graduated to APBA, a dice game that included strategic options and cards of major league players with numerical designations that were supposed to reflect their actual performance. I can remember my mother stepping over us as we spent rainy days playing on the floor of our house. She'd be praying that the weather would break so that we'd get out from under her feet.

But usually we played in Johnny's basement with its low-hung ceiling. We spent hours upon hours down there, including a good chunk of our winters. We established a league and kept statistics. Even then I enjoyed the decision making involved in managing and always maintained my cool in tight games. Now, Johnny—he was another story. Once he became so enraged at his starting pitcher that he took the player's card and stuck it under a faucet of running water. "I'm sending you to the showers!" he yelled. Johnny would get so furious after losing a hotly contested game that he'd fling the whole game off a table, sending pieces scattering across the basement floor. I'd just sit there and ask, "Are you through?" And then I'd pick up the pieces, place them back on the table, and quietly ask, "Are you ready for the next game?"

Even when I was as young as ten, I enjoyed the nuances of baseball more than anything, mostly because Frank had schooled me in the proper way to play the game. After a sandlot game I liked to talk to my friends about why we won or lost. They'd talk about a last-inning home run or a crucial error, but I'd always talk about little things—such as the way the outfielder threw to the wrong base, allowing a runner to advance to set up a run. That's one reason I enjoyed the 1996 World Series as much as I did, especially that classic ten-inning Game Four. Sitting in the trenches trying to run the other manager out of players, while at the same time trying to keep an ace in the hole yourself—that's the kind of game where a manager can really influence the outcome. There were so many twists and turns in that Series that had nothing to do with hitting home runs.

At an early age I was in love with the game and all its splendid intricacies, the way someone else might fall for a girl and love every single feature about her, right down to the way she laughs. In fact, I had little time for girls growing up. The combination of my devotion to baseball and my awkward shyness assured that I was one of a vanishing breed of Americans that stayed a virgin through all his teenage years. Frank found that out in 1956. I was fifteen when he invited me to join him in Milwaukee for two weeks. I took an airplane ride for the first time in my life. On the second leg of the trip, leaving from an airport in Indiana or Ohio or someplace, the airplane had engine trouble and had to turn back. I was scared as hell. When I finally got to Milwaukee, Frank introduced me to his roommate, Tommy Ferguson, who was the visiting clubhouse attendant at Milwaukee County Sta-

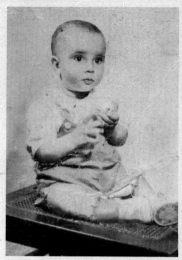

I was born Joseph Paul Torre on July 18, 1940, in Madison Park Hospital in Brooklyn, the first of my parents' five children to be born in a hospital.

One year old, on a pony in front of our house.

The front of our house at 3322 Avenue T in Brooklyn. The house has been in our family since 1935. My sister Rae still lives there.

Sister Marguerite, my sister, playing with me on our front stoop. She grew up with the name Josephine but changed it, as is the tradition, once she entered the convent.

Sitting between my two sisters, Sister Marguerite and Rae, who always doted on me.

Here I am, between my parents, at my brother Rocco's wedding in 1951. I remember this as my last skinny summer.

In Denver, Colorado, visiting with Frank. It would take me years and years of teasing before I lost the weight I gained in Denver.

I have always looked up to my brother Frank. This is Frank and me posing with some of his baseball trophies.

Frank, who was on his way to playing professional ball, ensured that I would start playing the game early. Rocco, who was in the Navy, was responsible for the Navy suit.

Thirteen years old, holding my nephew Robert in Rocco's apartment on Winthrop Street in Brooklyn. Robert had been at all the New York games during the 1996 World Series and at my house for the celebration after. He passed away suddenly in January 1997.

My eighth-grade graduation photo from P.S. 207.

The family out in Blue Point, Long Island, to visit Sister Marguerite at the convent. *From left to right:* Rae, Dad, Sister Marguerite, Rocco, Mom, and me.

My friends and I at the Copacabana the night of Johnny Parascandola's senior prom. Johnny is on my left.

This photograph ran in the New York papers on May 22, 1956, under the headline "Frank's Back With the Home Folks." Frank, already a hometown hero, was with the Braves, and they were in Brooklyn to play the Dodgers. *From left to right:* Rae, Rocco, Mom, me, and Frank. (INTERNATIONAL NEWS SOUND/PHOTO)

All my children came to celebrate Christmas 1996. *From left to right:* Michael's wife, Dayna, Lauren holding her daughter Kendra, Michael, me holding Andrea Rae, Lauren's husband, Gianni, and Cristina.

dium and who, like Frank, was single. "Tommy says you can work in the clubhouse if you want," my brother said, "shining shoes and hanging up jocks." It sounded like paradise to me. Frank, though, was the kind of brother who wanted to cover every end of my life. He figured I was at an age when my hormones were kicking in. So he arranged to set me up with one of his old girlfriends in Milwaukee, a bombshell of a blonde. I told my brother I wasn't interested; I was too busy working for Tommy. That wasn't the only reason, of course. I was afraid I wouldn't know what to do with a woman. I was still so shy and embarrassed about myself, I didn't dare take my brother up on his offer. To this day Frank likes to say I was more interested in hanging up jocks than in getting together with a beautiful blonde. And he was right. I wasn't exactly proud of my physique in those days either. I wasn't too thrilled to let my buddies or Frank's teammates see my body, let alone one of his old girlfriends. I just didn't have the confidence. Besides, what could be better than being at a ballpark?

Seeing Frank at the ballpark was always a thrill for me. Our whole family was so proud when he phoned with the news that he had been called up to the big leagues in 1956. Sister Marguerite was semicloistered in a convent in Blue Point, Long Island, at the time. The place was run by a very strict humorless Mother Vicar, who was from Belgium and spoke English with a very thick accent. Sister

Marguerite had warned me about her whenever our family would go to visit. She'd say, "Now, Joey, don't laugh when she says something, because she's going to think you're laughing at her."

So our family was visiting Sister Marguerite right after Frank had been called up by the Braves. We were chatting about it when the Mother Vicar came ambling over to us, the rosary beads rattling in her hands. "Oh, now the Torre family is all excited," she said. "What is going on?"

"Well, Mother Vicar," Sister Marguerite said, "we're excited because Frank was taken up into the major leagues."

"Oh, my dear," she said. "Does that mean he's going to be playing against Notre Dame?"

I would have broken out in hysterical laughter, except I remembered how my sister asked me not to laugh around the Mother Vicar. I nearly burst my spleen keeping that laugh inside me.

One of the great perks to having a brother in the big leagues, besides getting the chance to hang out with ballplayers before games, was having them actually visit the house. Frank made sure to bring teammates to our house to eat whenever the Braves played in New York. I remember guys like Johnny Logan and Chuck Cottier and Eddie Mathews coming over to our house. My mother would bring out a large antipasto platter, and the guys would dig in. Then she'd bring out the lasagna, and they'd all stuff themselves. And then she'd bring out the roast beef and chicken, and they'd look at each other like

"What's this for?" They thought they were finished with the meal after the lasagna. Wrong. My mother would make a six-course meal and, naturally, insist that they eat most of it. Those guys would wind up lying uncomfortably all over the floor in our house, completely stuffed.

Little brothers are known to pester their older brothers and friends with all kinds of idiotic questions, especially if their older brother's friends are big leaguers. But it was just the opposite for me. I was afraid to open my mouth around them. I'd listen intently as they talked about everything from the pitchers they batted against to their favorite restaurants on the road. But I'd always be too embarrassed to ask any questions. I was the same way in school. There were many questions I wanted to ask, but I was afraid of asking one stupid question, so I kept my mouth shut. I always admired the kid who asked the stupid question that I wanted to ask because at least he had the courage to do it.

Like Frank, I brought friends home for meals too—friends from the sandlots and, later, the big leagues. My mother was a terrific cook who kept the place stocked with food, as if she had to be ready with the necessary provisions for a great flood or snowstorm that would keep everyone housebound for weeks. The house always was open to friends and always for a full meal. She'd never just say, "Here, fix yourself a sandwich." She kept at least a dozen or so steaks in a freezer in the basement. I'd bring some of my friends over to the house after playing a sandlot game, and Mom would dig out five or six steaks for us. After she cooked them in the basement over an old stove, she'd put the steaks on a hand rack and turn them over an open flame to give them a barbecued taste.

One day when I was about eighteen I brought home a chubby friend of mine from Manhattan named Tony. We both loved music and enjoyed talking about our favorite rock-and-roll singers of those days. Of course, my mom filled him with food every time he stopped by. A number of years later, when I was managing the Braves, I got a call in spring training from him, saying, "This is Tony Orlando. How come you never ask me over to the house anymore?" Until then I just never realized that that chubby kid from Manhattan was the same Tony Orlando who became a big-time singer.

Playing baseball kept me out of serious trouble when I was a kid. I had great respect for my mom and never wanted to embarrass the family in any way. Moreover, Rocco was a police officer in Brooklyn, so I knew the importance of staying on the right side of the law. I still had Rae's streak of honesty in me to keep me in line. When I did find trouble, it was more mischievous than anything else. One time I was with Johnny and a few other guys when we stole one of those street barricades, the kind with a yellow flashing light atop a sawhorse. We tried hiding it under our jackets as we transported it as inconspicuously as possible to our block, wondering if we could actually divert traffic so we could play without being interrupted by cars. I don't remember what happened to the traffic flow, but I remember that we were such honest thieves that we felt obligated to return the barricade the next day, prompting us to stage a repeat of our charade: a bunch of kids trying to move around a big flashing light atop a sawhorse without anyone noticing.

That was about the extent of my delinquency, hardly the kind of material TV cop shows look for. I wasn't a drinker either. I'd have a beer now and then, although I never liked the taste. At home I drank some red wine mixed with cola. Other than that, I drank only on those rare momentous social occasions when you thought you were supposed to drink—like at the prom. I remember going to Johnny's prom for James Madison High. I attended with a girl named Dorothy Bortko. Johnny took one of my former girlfriends, Elisa Castellon. In those days there was no Verrazano Bridge between Brooklyn and Staten Island; only ferry service. The real "in" thing to do on prom night was to ride the ferry in the early morning hours—drinking and, if you happened to be supremely confident and lucky, necking with your date—after spending the evening at a nightclub. After we hung out at the Copacabana, we headed to the ferry. Johnny and some of the other guys had the booze. I was entrusted with the shot glasses. As I jumped onto the ferry, one of the shot glasses escaped from under the cover of my jacket and broke apart on the deck with a resounding crash that I imagined matched the decibel output of the A-bomb. The ferry people, with a wink, let us on anyway. It wasn't long before Johnny was teetering along the edge of the ferry—not exactly a wise maneuver in the middle of the night, especially for someone who couldn't swim. I advised him he'd better get his feet firmly back on the deck. That was typical of me. I had my moments of being irresponsible, but for the most part I was a pretty serious kid who was aware of what was dangerous and what wasn't.

Even though baseball helped me stay in line, we didn't have Little League when I was growing up, so I had to organize my own team. The most renowned sandlot team in Brooklyn was the Brooklyn Cadets, which began playing in 1944 and, with Frank's help, won a national tournament in 1949. The Cadets were like the Yankees in those days; they won the city title almost every year. I was ready to be a Cadet when I was twelve years old. The problem was, you weren't allowed to play until you were in high school. So I asked the coach, Dan Hill, if he had any old uniforms that my friends and I could wear so we could be just like the big kids. Hill said sure he did. So we'd get dressed up in these oversize Cadets uniforms and drum up some games, even though we weren't part of an official league.

Two years later, in 1954, I enrolled at St. Francis Prep, an all-boys parochial high school with about eleven hundred students in downtown Brooklyn.

The rest of my family had attended public high school. When Frank paid the tuition, he said to me, "I want to make sure you really want to go there, and not just because your sister is a nun."

"Yeah, I want to go," I said. A good friend of mine from up the street, Bob Finelli, went to St. Francis, and it seemed like the fun thing to do.

It wasn't. I'm sure the education was great. But I quickly found out that the brothers who taught at the school thought nothing of whacking you with an open hand or a ruler. One of my teachers, Brother Charles, used to smack kids with a drumstick. I was so nervous around those teachers that I played hooky often, spending the day riding the trains. I just didn't want to go to school. Years later after the Prep went coed and moved to Flushing, Sister Marguerite wound up teaching at St. Francis. On one of her first days there she found herself in the bookstore talking with a brother who worked in the attendance office. When he found out who she was, he blurted out loud enough for the whole store to hear, "Ooooh, that brother of yours! Has he straightened himself out yet?" I wasn't exactly a bookish kind of kid in the first place, and once I missed a day of classes here and there, I was clueless. It was a dead-end street. I look back on it now and realize how stupid I was to miss those classes and fall behind like that.

My high school years were not the best of times. The truth is that I had no confidence in myself. I didn't do anything, join any clubs or anything like that. I didn't even play baseball until my junior year. I think I tried out for baseball one time during my sophomore year but didn't feel confident enough to go ahead with it. I was a champion of self-defeat. I was this shy, overweight kid and didn't believe I had the skills or, especially, the confidence to play high school baseball. I didn't pull the ball—I hit naturally to center field and right field—and I thought that was a detriment. (It turned out to be a huge asset for me as a professional. It's much easier to hit when you can hit the ball to all fields.) Besides, when I was in high school my brother was on his way to the big leagues. I figured, how many families have *two* guys in the big leagues? I think back to the way I was, and it's too bad I didn't get involved more in high school.

In the summer after my freshman year, however, I did work up enough courage to join the Cadets, which really wasn't that hard to do because a bunch of my friends played with them. The Cadets played more than a hundred games each year over several different leagues. We played two or three nights during the week, doubleheaders on Saturdays and tripleheaders on Sundays, starting at nine-thirty in the morning. I remember I had to go to six-thirty mass on Sunday mornings, and I'd see people still dressed in Saturday night's clothes—staggering in sleepless from proms, weddings, or whatever.

That first season, playing in the freshman division for the Cadets, I was named the league's most valuable player while playing first base and pitcher, an honor I'd attain the next year as well. I also began to show further signs, that first year, of my future managerial skills. A couple of our players missed a practice right before one of our championship games, so our coach, Jim McElroy, suspended them. Many of the other guys got together and made some noise about not playing in the game unless the suspended players were reinstated. Here were fourteen- and fifteen-year-old kids discussing a strike of a championship game. I pulled the team together and said, "Listen, when we joined this team, we made a commitment to this team, and it's up to all of us to live up to it. It's our responsibility to play this game and for Coach McElroy to suspend those guys if he has to." I must have been persuasive—or maybe the guys were just chicken about going ahead with a strike—because we did play and the suspensions did stick. We wound up losing.

We played most of our games at the Parade Grounds in Brooklyn. The Parade Grounds included thirteen diamonds, only two of which had enclosed fences and stands. The rest were very ragged, dusty fields jammed together back to back. They had damn near flat mounds and clouds of dust with every step you took. With my shape in those days, I looked like a tumbleweed whenever I rambled around the bases. But the thirteen diamonds were almost always filled, especially during the weekends. The games at the enclosed fields drew large crowds, often with big league scouts included.

In addition to Frank and me, other big leaguers who came out of the Parade Grounds included Sandy Koufax, Joe Pepitone, Rusty Torres, Bob Aspromonte, Matt Galante, Frank Tepedino, and Don McMahon. I don't think they play as much ball there these days, but some of the more recent Parade Grounds graduates include Manny Ramirez of the Cleveland Indians and Frankie Rodriguez of the Minnesota Twins.

My mother came to some of my games, just as she had done with Rocco and Frank. She'd sit there in the stands clutching her rosary beads tightly in her hands, and she'd shoot the nastiest looks you could imagine to anyone who dared bring any kind of dishonor upon her sons, such as an opposing pitcher who threw a little too far inside. No one could give dirty looks like my mother. She didn't yell much during the game—she'd pretty much just be saying her rosary and throwing dirty looks. She was the same way when I got to the big leagues. Her support meant so much to me that I came up with a way to acknowledge her presence, whether she was at the game or watching on television. I told her that before every at bat I would take my helmet off and wipe my brow. That would be our little signal. And I did it every time I knew she was watching me at the plate. That was my way of saying hello and thanking her for all of her years of support and love.

During my second season with the Cadets, 1956, I stood about six foot one, weighed 240 pounds, and had a forty-inch waist. I turned sixteen that year. I was just about as wide as I was tall. Opposing teams took one look at me—this huge kid with a serious five o'clock shadow—and immediately complained to the umpire that I was way too old to be playing in that league. Jim McElroy took to traveling around with my birth certificate. Anytime we played someone who didn't know us, Jim would have to whip out that birth certificate and show it to the umpire.

After two MVP seasons with the Cadets, I finally convinced myself to play baseball at St. Francis Prep, starting in 1957. I did well playing first and third base, and I even pitched. I remember one home run I hit at Brooklyn Prep that cleared the fence and broke a window in the school. You don't forget those kinds of dingers. We had a left-handed pitcher who started calling me Joe Toots that year—I think because of all the chattering I did in the infield. I was always saying, "Come on, babe! Come on, toots!" Guys just started calling me Toots for short.

Sadly, that's something that's disappeared from baseball—all that infield chatter. It just doesn't happen anymore. Players today have less fun on the field than players of my generation did. The huge amounts of money involved have turned the game more into a business. In the big leagues I liked to talk on the field, especially when I was catching. I really enjoyed talking to hitters when they came up to the plate. I'd talk about baseball, restaurants, golf, whatever. I guess it drove some players nuts, like Tim McCarver. Timmy was wired a lot differently from me, when I first entered the league. He was a guy who fought himself, who thought he should get a hit every time up. Paul O'Neill and Tino Martinez are the same way. Later on Timmy and I would become not just teammates but really good friends. But one day in Atlanta in 1967, when he was playing with the Cardinals, he came up to me before a game and said, "Joe, look, I don't know what you're trying to do, but it really pisses me off when you talk to me in the batter's box. I'd really appreciate it if you didn't say anything to me." I just nodded to him.

The first time McCarver came up, I reminded him, "Now I won't say anything, just like you asked."

"Good," he growled.

I dropped into my crouch and put down a sign for Denny Lemaster, our pitcher that day. Everything was dead quiet, like McCarver wanted it. Just as Lemaster went into his windup to throw the ball, I broke the tense silence by blurting out, "I promise! I won't say a thing!" McCarver burst out in such a big laugh that there was no way he could swing the bat. The ball sailed past him for a strike. To this day he says he never laughed so hard and so sincerely during a baseball game.

I remember another game when I was catching for the Braves and Wade Blasingame was pitching against Houston. Blasingame hung a curveball to

Rusty Staub so badly that as it was floating toward the plate, I said, "Oh, no!" Just as I feared he would, Rusty crushed it for a home run. As Rusty crossed home plate, he gave me a glance and said, "Oh, yes!"

At St. Francis Prep I turned out to be an even better hitter than I was a talker. Rocco's police assignments one summer were at Coney Island. He'd make sure the owners of the bat-a-way cages would allow me to hit for free. I'd hit until my hands broke open with blood. I'd hit the ball so far and hard that people would stop what they were doing and watch. The elevated subway train would pass by what would have been the outfield at those cages. I know I hit some balls over the train cars as they rumbled by, and they must have been three hundred feet away. Even one of the brothers at St. Francis Prep began to notice my hitting prowess. Brother Regis was the Latin teacher who gave students a healthy whack if they did something egregious like forgetting homework or missing class. But he would say to me, "When I come over to you and it looks like I'm going to do something, just yell, 'Baseball!' " The guy spared me a few licks.

Unfortunately, major league scouts didn't take as kindly to me. I never heard from any of them my senior year in high school, even though I hit about .500. Frank, though, did hear from at least one scout. I had pushed Frank to find out what the scouts thought of me, so he finally contacted somebody he knew with the Boston Red Sox. The scout sent back a telegram to Frank that said, "Not only is he not a major league prospect, he's not even a professional prospect." Everyone agreed: I was too fat and too slow to be a ballplayer. No one wanted me.

I later heard that Al Campanis, then a scout for the Dodgers, received a telephone call from someone that he should check out this certain first baseman–pitcher from St. Francis Prep. Campanis, who had signed Koufax out of Brooklyn under similar circumstances, decided to watch me play. He later summed up his report this way: "I couldn't believe it. The kid weighed about 245 pounds, and the other club knocked him out in the first inning. He went to first base and showed absolutely no coordination there. I turned the kid down flat."

Even my brother's team, the Braves, didn't want me. Milwaukee farm director John Mullen called up Honey Russell, the same scout who signed Frank, to ask about me. Russell had been scouting me for a while. "Forget it," Russell told him. "He's a fat kid with no speed to play first base or third base." It didn't even help when I played great for the Cadets that year. I won the batting title at the 1958 All-American Amateur Baseball Association tournament in Johnstown, Pennsylvania, with a .647 average. (Frank had won the same batting title in 1949, making us the only two brothers to accomplish the feat.)

So instead of going off to play professional baseball somewhere, after I graduated from St. Francis I got a job working as a page on the American Stock Exchange. I earned thirty-three dollars a week. I still played baseball with the Cadets then. In fact, Frank had arranged through Jim McElroy to move me to the Brooklyn Royals, a team that played in a higher division than the Cadets. He figured the better competition would help me. However, I told them no thanks, that I'd prefer to continue to play with my friends. Jim always thought that showed a great deal of loyalty and humility. The truth was, it had more to do with my shyness. I wanted to stay around the people I knew.

I don't know what would have happened if I had stayed in the business of stocks and bonds. I liked the competitiveness of that arena. I liked the excitement on the floor—and the market was going crazy at the time. In fact, even after I made the big leagues, I would sell municipal bonds in the off-season. But as a high school graduate, I didn't know much and made my usual share of greenhorn mistakes, like the time I gave my family a tip to buy this great Cuban oil stock. Only Frank listened to me and bought some shares of United Cuban Oil. A short time later the government of Cuba was overthrown. Frank was none too happy about that. What I do know is that a tip from Frank that next year, 1959, changed my entire life.

Frank called up Jim McElroy before the start of the Cadets' season and said, "Jimmy, I want Joe to be a catcher. And as much as I want Joe to keep up the tradition and play for the Cadets, if you don't use him as a catcher, I'm going to put him on another team." Fortunately for me, the kid who had been catching for the Cadets was called into the service, so Jim agreed to switch me to catcher. Frank had a couple of reasons for wanting me to catch. First of all, I didn't have the body or the speed to play any other position as a professional. And second, he thought I was a candy-assed kid who needed to be toughened up. He hated the fact that I was the baby of the family whom my mother constantly coddled, calling me "my Joey" all the time. What better way to learn how to be tough than by taking foul tips off your body and getting run over by speeding base runners?

Actually, I liked catching right away, mostly because Frank sold me on the fact that it was the quickest way to the big leagues. I knew that not a lot of people wanted to catch, you didn't have to hit a great deal, and you didn't have to run fast. It sounded perfect to me.

Later that summer the Cadets were getting ready to go back to another All-American Amateur Baseball tournament in Johnstown. At the same time a firm on the American Exchange called Mann, Farrell, Jacoby and Green had plans for me: They wanted me to be a specialist clerk, which meant I would provide direct assistance to the broker on transactions. They would send me to school to be trained and would pay me if I was called into the service or the reserves. It was a full-time commitment. I'd have to give up baseball. I said, "Sorry,

I'm going to the Johnstown tournament." I didn't tell the Exchange when I left for the tournament, so they fired me. I tried to collect unemployment, but they wouldn't allow it because they said I got myself fired, which was hard to argue. Big deal. How much unemployment was I going to get after making only thirty-three bucks a week?

I hit terribly at Johnstown, batting a buck-thirty or something. But by then the scouts were starting to see me in a whole new light. Suddenly, as a catcher, I had become a real prospect. Several clubs were interested in me, including the Giants, Cubs, and Braves. Honey Russell, in fact, called up John Mullen and said, "I want to give Joe Torre a five-figure bonus."

"What? What the hell happened?" Mullen said, remembering how Russell had flatly rejected me the previous year.

"He's catching now," Russell said, "and he looks great there."

St. John's University also wanted me and was prepared to give me a scholarship. I wanted no part of anything to do with books though. I decided what it would take a club to sign me: enough money to pay off the mortgage on my mother's house and to buy myself a brand-new Chevrolet Impala, which was *the* hot car at the time. For some reason Frank wanted me to sign with the Cubs. I guess he figured Chicago had the most pressing need for a catcher. After all, his team, the Braves, had perennial all-star Del Crandall behind the plate. So the scout from the Cubs, Ralph DiLullo, presented his club's offer to my brother. Frank told him he was six thousand dollars short. DiLullo countered by saying he had reached his limit and wouldn't go back to his superviser to ask for more. The Giants offered even less than Chicago.

The Braves came through with what I wanted: $22,500 and a promise to send me to their Instructional League team in Florida that fall. As Frank likes to say, he had no choice but to let me sign with Milwaukee. So in August 1959 I signed my first contract. I was a professional baseball player. And I was a proud member of the same organization as my brother—not that my signing exactly sent squeals of delight through the Milwaukee front office.

The Braves' general manager, John McHale, called up Honey Russell and barked, "Why did you sign him? He looks like a boy bartender!"

Said Russell, "He'll be a better ballplayer than Frank."

I didn't know it at the time, but Frank had no problem telling other people the same thing. He'd say, "I'm nothing. Wait until you see my brother." Of course, he wouldn't lavish such praise on me when I was present. But the times I did get a small compliment from Frank—because he was so hard on me—meant more to me than any trophy or newspaper headline could.

With my bonus money I immediately paid off the mortgage on our house. I didn't get around to buying my car until the following year. By then I had cooled somewhat on the Impala, especially when Frank suggested I might get a good deal on a Ford through one of his many connections. Frank used to smoke cigars and play cards with a big car dealer in Milwaukee who gave special rates to Braves players. He put me in touch with the dealer's son, an eager young executive. I met him in the fall of 1960, when the 1961 models were coming out. He wanted to sell me a 1961 Thunderbird, but I explained how I preferred the look of the 1960 model, and we quickly worked out a deal. He was very easy to bargain with. He seemed very enthusiastic about selling a car to a ballplayer from New York. He explained that he was a big baseball fan who had grown up idolizing Joe DiMaggio. And that's how I wound up buying my first car, a 1960 T-Bird, from the future commissioner of baseball, Bud Selig.

CHAPTER 4

Destination: Milwaukee

IN SEPTEMBER 1959, ONE MONTH AF-
ter signing with Milwaukee at the age of nineteen, I telephoned Frank, who was playing with
the Braves. I was a little worried. "Frank, I know
the Instructional League is supposed to be starting
soon," I said, "and I haven't heard anything from
the Braves."

"Let me see what's going on," he said. My
brother went to the Milwaukee club offices to see
John McHale, the general manager, and John Mullen, the farm director.

"What are you guys doing?" Frank said in his
usual diplomatic style. "My brother is supposed to
be down in the Instructional League, and he hasn't
heard from anybody."

"Well," McHale said, "we feel he'd be overmatched down there. The competition's too good for him. So we decided against sending him there."

"Now you wait a minute," Frank said. "This organization made a commitment to this kid. It was a promise. And I'm telling you, if I have to go right to the owner of this team, my brother is going to the Instructional League."

Frank, as usual, was persistent and persuasive. The Braves reluctantly agreed to send me to the Instructional League. I had lost some of my baby fat by then. I really had expected to be signed out of high school, so when it didn't happen, it snapped some sense into me. I knew I had to be more careful about my weight. However, I still weighed a robust 220 pounds when I entered the Instructional League in Florida. Mullen took one look at me and said, "You gotta get some of that fat off you." He came back three weeks later and said proudly, "See that? Now you look good." I didn't have the heart to tell him that I actually had *gained* five pounds since he saw me and was up to 225. But I think I looked in better shape just from the daily grind of catching. I was getting stronger. My body was getting firmer.

I started out catching only once every fourth day in the Instructional League, a league that included the top prospects of every organization. By the time the league ended, I was catching every other day and playing the outfield on the other days. I think it's safe to say I proved to the Braves that I was not overmatched. I wound up leading the whole damned league in hitting with a .364 batting average. My confidence soared. I knew heading into that league that I had above-average ability. I knew I had quick hands at the plate, and I had always been the best player on my block in Brooklyn. But now I knew that I belonged as a professional ballplayer. I still wasn't nearly as confident off the field—I was still shy and chubby—but I felt at ease on the diamond.

A few months later, in February 1960, I unofficially reported to the Braves' spring training camp in Bradenton, Florida.

It was a little strange being there. I knew many of the Braves from my summer vacations visiting Frank in Milwaukee or from working out with them before games at Ebbets Field. But now I was a professional myself, and I had to go out and perform. At least I was in better shape since the last time most of the Braves had seen me. Warren Spahn took one look at me and said, "This can't be the same fat kid!" After a week or two, the Braves assigned me to a training complex in Waycross, Georgia. This kid who had grown up on the asphalt streets of Brooklyn amid sewers and stoops found himself amid swampy fields and snakes. You had to be careful while shagging balls into the outfield during batting practice. If you chased a ball deep into that murky field, you would come across some of those healthy-sized creatures. I wasn't much of a naturalist, but I guess I did show them something with the bat. My teammates found themselves tiptoeing through the high grass to retrieve my home run balls almost daily.

The Braves decided to assign me to one of their two Class C teams, which I figured was better than going to Class D, the lowest rung on the pro baseball ladder. The C teams were in Boise, Idaho, and Eau Claire, Wisconsin. The Braves sent me to Eau Claire, in the Northern League, because its manager, Bill Steinecke, was a former catcher and would be able to tutor me. He taught me mostly the old-school stuff about blocking the plate and, if you got banged up, just to spit on it and keep playing. Steinecke was a grizzled, gruff, tobacco-spitting old goat. I remember after games we'd take showers in this tiny room—no bigger than a closet—with three nozzles. You'd be taking a shower, and all of a sudden you'd feel something warm on your leg. It was Steinecke pissing on you. Steinecke's lessons were straight from the school of hard knocks. Those lessons actually underscored some of the same things I had heard from Frank, who wanted me to be more assertive. It was Frank who ingrained in me how important it is to have the people who play alongside you respect you. And the only way for that to happen is to go out there and play hard every day.

Eau Claire was a complete joy for me. You hear a lot of horror stories about players adjusting to their first minor league season—guys getting homesick, putting up with terrible living conditions and long bus rides—but I thoroughly enjoyed my time in

Eau Claire. I lived with two other players in the house of an elderly couple. The three of us shared a room. The couple charged each of us five dollars per week, which was very reasonable for a guy pulling down four hundred a month to play ball. The wife was nicknamed Strawberry because of her strawberry blond hair. She used to make us coffee and breakfast in the morning and come to every one of our home games, yelling in her deep strong voice and clanging a cowbell. She called all of the players PT-ers, for pants tearers, because she thought we were all girl crazy and couldn't wait to tear the pants off the local beauties. "Go out and get all the girls, you PT-ers," she'd say. Strawberry was great. She was like having a mom away from home.

Eau Claire was a pretty suburban city with a pretty ballpark. Our team traveled in shiny red Chevrolet station wagons with the Braves' Indian logo painted on the side door. We all took turns driving, covering many miles, mostly at night. The worst trip of all was to Minot, North Dakota—an expedition of about six hundred miles. We stuffed all the baseball gear into a trailer and hooked it up to one of the wagons, which made driving that vehicle particularly difficult. You'd find yourself dozing off at the wheel sometimes. When you snapped yourself awake, you inevitably caused the wagon to swerve, and you'd look in the rearview mirror and see the trailer swaying back and forth like a fish, threatening to go crashing off the road with all the bats, balls, and equipment.

When we played in Fargo, North Dakota, we actually stayed across the state line in Moorhead, Minnesota, which was weird because Moorhead time was an hour ahead of Fargo. More than a few guys were confused when we tried to figure out what time we were supposed to be at the ballpark. The worst part was coming back to the motel after the game, because we lost an hour just on the ride back; we couldn't get anything to eat. Talk about bad eating habits—we hit more hamburger stands than doubles that season.

We played in other places such as Winnipeg, Manitoba; Aberdeen, South Dakota; and St. Cloud, Minnesota. The games could get heated because everyone from the players to the umpires was fighting his way to the big leagues. I had several up-close-and-personal confrontations in that league with future National League umpire Bruce Froemming. He threw me out of games six times that summer. I hated him, and he hated me. We both were young and had quick tempers. I'd complain about a pitch when I was catching, and he would scream back at me. Being the spoiled kid that I was, I'd scream back at him. Of course, he would always get the last word; he'd run me from the game. Usually he'd follow up on that by tossing Steinecke out of the game too. The Braves wanted to punish me for being so hot-headed by sending me to D ball. When Steinecke, who saw me crushing the ball all summer, heard about that, he said, "Why don't you send the kid to Triple-A instead?" He thought I belonged in a higher league, but I stayed in Eau Claire. Some people might have a hard time believing that I had such a short fuse then. Actually, I still have a temper now. The difference is I have more patience. It's just been a matter of growing up. And believe me, I took a long time to grow up.

As for Mr. Froemming, I guess his job is not as conducive to mellowing as mine. He's still a good umpire who likes to scream, and he's actually become a good friend as well. One day in the late 1970s, when I was managing the Mets through the course of yet another hopelessly lost game, I decided I'd try to fire up the club by getting myself thrown out. I don't even remember what the argument was about, but I ran out there to Froemming between second base and third base and was getting started with my expletive-filled act. But Bruce was too smart. "I know why you're out here," he said. "You're out here to get thrown out of the game. And you know what? I'm not going to do it. No matter what you say."

"Well," I said, "I might as well take the opportunity to do this," after which I proceeded to call him every name in the book, especially those magic words that otherwise earn you an automatic expulsion. By the time I gave it up and left the field— still in the game, of course—I was laughing.

My first professional season, Froemming notwithstanding, was a huge success. I won the Northern League batting title by hitting .344. I banged out six hits in a doubleheader on the final day of the season to edge Max Alvis. I also finished with 16 home runs and 74 runs batted in over 117 games, made the all-star team, and was named the league's rookie of the year. I even stole seven bases, a modest total that I'd never again duplicate on any level. The worst part of that year was when the Braves demoted Frank to Louisville, one of their Triple-A teams. I was shocked. Frank was twenty-nine years old, had been in the big leagues for four and a half years, and had played on two pennant winners, and the next thing you know he's back in the minors. Looking back, that wasn't so unusual in those days—not with only sixteen teams in all of major league baseball. Competition for jobs was fierce, nothing like what you have today, where guys can easily hang on. Back then you had fewer major league teams and more levels of minor league clubs.

When my season ended, I headed to Milwaukee, where Frank maintained a home, to wait for him to come back from Louisville when his season ended. When I arrived in Milwaukee, I received a message to go see John McHale. I had no idea what it was about. I was stunned when he gave me the news: They were calling me up to the big leagues. It was a thrill just to be in that clubhouse and be getting dressed with all those great players. It really helped me that I knew most of the Braves players already; I wasn't as much in awe of the situation as I might have been otherwise.

My only regret was that Frank wasn't there with the Braves when I broke in. My timing, never one of my better traits, was the slightest bit off. We had missed each other by about three months, with Frank going down to the minors while I was on my way up. We played against each other later, in 1962 and 1963 when Frank was with Philadelphia, but we never played on the same team, except in spring training. Frank had had more to do with getting me to the big leagues than anybody else, so I would have loved to share the experience with him.

My promotion happened so fast and so unexpectedly that no one in my family saw my big league debut. People just didn't hop on a plane then as they do now. On September 25, 1960, I was sitting on the bench in Milwaukee, and left-hander Harvey Haddix of the Pirates was beating us 3–1 in the ninth inning. All of a sudden our manager, Charlie Dressen, yelled out, "Torre!" He wanted me to hit for Warren Spahn. I grabbed a bat and stepped in the batter's box. My legs were actually shaking. I figured I might as well just look for a fastball and hope to get some wood on it. The first pitch was a ball. Then Haddix threw me a fastball away, and I hit it up the middle for a base hit. When I got to first base, I was feeling on top of the world—until I looked over and saw they were sending out a pinch runner for me, Lee Maye. I didn't even get the ball as a souvenir. I didn't even think about it at the time. Now rookies and veterans alike routinely stop games to claim the baseball from every milestone hit they get.

A few days later in Pittsburgh, Dressen used me

as a pinch hitter again. This time Bob Friend, a right-handed pitcher, threw me a slider and two curveballs. That was it. I was soup, striking out on three pitches. My batting average went from 1.000 to .500, which is where it stayed for the rest of the season as I had no more at bats. When I came home to Avenue T, I was the hero of the neighborhood. It was only the previous summer that I had been playing for a sandlot team and catching for the first time in my life, and now here I was, a real big league player with a real big league hit to my credit. The best part was thinking about all those games of APBA baseball I played with Johnny Parascandola in his basement—all those big league ballplayers we pretended to be, through the magic of cards and dice. Now I was one of those guys. Even now, twenty years after my playing career has ended, every once in a while somebody writing to me for an autograph will enclose my own APBA card. Whenever I see one, it's like opening an old photo album.

After the 1960 season the Braves sent me back to the Instructional League to continue to work on my catching skills. I had the worst luck there. I developed a stiff throwing shoulder that kept me out of action for a few days. I wrote a letter to Johnny Parascandola telling him about it but asked that he not tell my mother. I didn't want her to worry about me getting hurt, because I knew she still thought of me as her baby. But really I was embarrassed about how it happened. I had been wading in a swimming pool, then come home and taken a nap with no shirt on in front of an air conditioner. (I've worn a shirt to bed ever since.) I also came down with tonsillitis and the flu there, which turned out to be a blessing in disguise. I lost about twenty pounds, dropping to 195. But when I went home to Mom's cooking, I quickly put the weight back on.

After one year of professional baseball, I was a training-camp holdout the next spring. There were no player agents in those days. I was getting my advice from Frank. The Braves offered to pay me six hundred dollars a month. I wanted a thousand. After my brief holdout of a few days, I agreed to play for eight hundred. Best of all, Milwaukee invited me to my first big league camp. It was the only time Frank and I played together, not including the stickball games on Avenue T. It meant so much to me to have the opportunity to play with him. In those days teams played a lot of split squad games, known as B games, and usually those games were on the road. The Braves would throw together a B squad consisting mostly of guys the club didn't have to find out about or didn't care to find out about. That's how I wound up playing a lot that spring with guys like Frank, Wes Covington, Johnny Logan, Billy Martin, and Warren Spahn.

One day Frank and I were driving to the Braves' training complex in my new T-Bird. I had had it out of Bud Selig's showroom for only a few months. I was approaching an intersection in the right lane as the light turned green. I passed a large truck that was stopped in the left lane. All of a sudden Frank yelled, "Watch out!" A man was driving through the red light on the other side of the truck. He struck my T-Bird on the front side. The car was totaled. We had no serious injuries, though Frank did suffer some nagging shoulder and back injuries that shortened his career.

Frank and I talked all the time that spring— we'd sit together on the team bus, and he would correct me during games. I'd come back to the dugout after an at bat, and he'd say something like "Did you know with two strikes that you move closer to the plate?" And I'd say, "Yeah. I did know that." That's Frank. He would be so aware of everything I did, no matter how subtle.

One day we were playing the Washington Senators in Pompano Beach. I was catching, Frank was playing first, and Spahn, whom everybody called Hooks, was pitching. Spahn kept shaking off my signs that day. Finally, after somebody smacked a curveball for a hit, I walked out to the mound. Naturally, Frank had to be there too.

"Curveball was not the pitch," Frank said to me. "We call him Hooks because of his nose, not because of his curveball."

Another time, during an intrasquad game, I blocked the plate against Frank and tagged him out. Frank got up from his slide cursing. It was tremendous fun playing that spring with him. I even had fun in later years playing against him when he was with the Phillies. Gene Mauch was the

Phillies' manager then. He would hold clubhouse meetings before games to review how to pitch to the opposing hitters. Whenever the Phillies played the Braves, Mauch would ask Frank, "How should we pitch to your brother?" And Frank would lay out his plan of attack to get me out. Then, after Frank went out on the field for batting practice, Mauch would call the pitchers and catchers back for a clandestine meeting. Mauch had convinced himself that Frank was setting him up, so he'd change the way they pitched me. The kicker is that I absolutely destroyed Philadelphia pitching in the years Mauch managed the team.

Despite the joy of spending so much time with Frank during that 1961 training camp, one of my most vivid memories from that time doesn't include my brother at all. I remember playing the Yankees in Bradenton. It was the first inning, and Mickey Mantle stepped into the batter's box. He wore a rubber jacket beneath his uniform to sweat off some of the pounds he'd gained over the winter. To me, this twenty-year-old kid squatting behind the plate, he looked absolutely enormous. He appeared, as he did to many people in those glory days, larger than life. Mickey Mantle, right there next to me. I got goose bumps. I don't remember what he did that day, but I'll never forget what I did. I nailed a pitch from Whitey Ford toward center field. I hit it pretty well, but I think the wind helped it a little. Mantle chased after it, but the ball carried over the wall. Some moments just stay with you in life; the images never lose their sharpness of focus or richness of color. This was one of them: a home run off Whitey Ford, with Mickey Mantle, his powerful legs giving up the chase, looking up at the baseball that I had hit as it flew away against the blue Florida sky. I've always wished I had a picture of that moment. But I guess I do.

That happened to be the first spring camp in which the Milwaukee Braves wanted every player on the team to stay together—black and white players alike. The South was very much still a segregated place then. In fact, the exclusive hotel in Bradenton where the team planned to stay wouldn't have us under those conditions, so we had to move out to the Twilight Motel in Palmetto, a neighboring town. And even there they had to feed us in a private room where no one else could see blacks and whites eating together. The whole thing just struck me as very, very strange. In Brooklyn there were blacks and whites and there were Jews and Italians—we were aware of our differences—but there never was any segregation. I just couldn't understand what was happening in the South. Segregation first struck me back in 1954, when I visited Frank while he was playing in Atlanta during his minor league days. I was a fourteen-year-old kid walking through the stands of Ponce de Leon Park when I saw a sign that said "Colored Water Fountain." And then I saw one that said "Colored Rest Rooms." I just didn't understand it. When the game started, I noticed that all the blacks were sitting in the outfield bleachers. They weren't allowed to sit in the stands with the whites. I said to myself, This doesn't make any sense. I had black kids in my high school, and they were treated the same as anybody else. I couldn't fathom why it would be so different in the South. It was like another planet.

I had a great spring in 1961: nine hits in 15 at bats, with four home runs and 11 runs batted in. I didn't expect to make the big club. After all, the Braves were set behind the plate with Del Crandall, an all-star who was only thirty years old. I wasn't surprised when they assigned me to Triple-A Louisville. The Braves also sent Frank to Triple-A. Unfortunately, they sent him to their team in Vancouver, where the roster was filled more with older players than with prospects. It felt kind of odd, because I think we both knew at that juncture that my career was in its ascension and that it was about to eclipse his. Frank was great about that, though. He continued to support me and encourage me—in his brusque manner—through our frequent telephone conversations. Frank was a very good hitter who could pull anybody's fastball. He talked to me a lot about the mechanics and strategies of hitting.

When the Braves sent me to Triple-A, Dressen, the manager, told some reporters, "We don't have to worry as much about a replacement for Crandall anymore. If anything happens to him, we'll send for Torre." Even Crandall was gracious, calling me "the best young catcher they've brought up to this club

87

since I've been here." It was in Louisville where I first met another catcher in the Braves' system who would become a lifelong friend and source of many moments of hilarity on and off the field: Bob Uecker. Bob had been my brother's roommate at Louisville the previous season, and now he was my backup. Uke was a real sweetheart who always kept things loose around the team.

One time Bob got his hands on some rocket fireworks. He buried them in a canister near the back wall of the bullpen, where he sat during games. When one of our players, Neil Chrisley, hit a home run, Bob lit the fuse. The fireworks left the ground when Chrisley touched second base and soared so high that they didn't explode until he hit third base. Streams of brightly colored lights fell to the field. Chrisley was so shocked he almost forgot to touch home plate. Uke proceeded to make his fireworks salute a Louisville tradition. The crowd loved it every time—but not everyone else did. Uke's pyrotechnics violated a local ordinance that prohibited loud noises after 10 P.M. John McHale traveled from Milwaukee to Louisville specifically to tell Uke to knock it off. Uke was a great guy to have on your club. Over our several years together in Louisville, Milwaukee, and Atlanta, Uke and I must have shared a million laughs.

Meanwhile, in spite of Uecker's distractions, I continued my hot hitting, especially during one road trip in May when I was getting hits all over the place. By May 19 I was hitting .342 and had knocked in twenty-four runs in twenty-seven games. That night after a game in Omaha, my manager at Louisville, Ben Geraghty, tried to reach me in my hotel room. Trouble was, I was in someone else's room playing cards. Geraghty finally tracked me down at about two in the morning in my room after I had been in bed for an hour.

"Get your things packed," Geraghty said. "You're catching a three thirty plane to Cincinnati."

I knew what that meant. I was going to the big leagues. Crandall had been bothered by a lingering problem in his throwing shoulder. His backup, Charlie Lau, who became a famous hitting coach, had been filling in, but now it looked as if Crandall would be out longer than the Braves first thought. I rushed off to the airport, only to find that my flight was delayed until 4:50 A.M. Because of that delay, I missed my 7:25 connection in Chicago by five minutes. The next plane left at ten o'clock. I arrived in Cincinnati forty-five minutes before the Braves' game against the Reds, so they didn't play me. They gave me uniform number 15. I was twenty years old and had only 144 games of minor league experience. As it turned out, I'd never play another game in the minors.

Warren Spahn was the starting pitcher for the first big league game I ever caught. He had been pitching in the big leagues for as long as I had lived. The old left-hander called me over before the

game and said, "Call your own game. If I don't
agree with the pitch you call, I'll shake you off."

There was one thing I felt most nervous about:
pop-ups. I had had trouble with them in the minors. The pop-ups would go above the height of the
lights in those minor league parks, and I'd lose
them for a moment. When they came down, too
often they did so on the ground behind me. Thankfully, this was a day game. Sure enough, a pop-up
went up behind the plate in the first inning. I saw
it right away and caught it easily. There—that was
what I needed. I was relaxed now. I had a great
doubleheader: a home run off Joey Jay, a double, a
single, and a circus catch of another foul pop-up
with two runners on. I also threw out Frank Robinson, Vada Pinson, and Eddie Kasko trying to steal
and, with a one-run lead in the ninth inning of the
second game, saved the win by tagging out Pinson
in a big collision at the plate.

Spahn, even though we lost the first game, shook
off my signs only three times. I thought that was
great—until I deduced later on that if Spahn didn't
like the signal, he'd just throw the pitch for a ball.
That's how good his control was. He was remark-
able. Later that season I had the great honor of
catching his three hundredth career win. The sad
part about Spahn's pitching was that when he had
his pinpoint control, the umpires would give him
pitches a little bit off the plate, but later in his
career when he started losing that precise control,

they stopped giving him those calls. And then it got ugly; he was hit hard.

Lew Burdette pitched the second game of that doubleheader. That was an experience, too, because Burdette was rumored to be a spitball pitcher. He told me before the game that he threw a "mystery pitch," and we worked out a sign for it. Burdette said I had to give him that sign quickly so that he had time to "prepare" to throw the pitch. A spitball breaks down so sharply that if you don't know it's coming, it's very difficult to catch. I found that out four years later, when I was catching Don Drysdale in the all-star game at Shea Stadium in New York. I knew Drysdale had a reputation for throwing a spitter, so I asked him before the game what sign I should use for it. He told me he didn't want me to use a sign; he'd just throw it sometimes when I called for a fastball. That didn't work so well. I wound up chasing it to the backstop three times. Burdette never told me or anybody else on the team what substance he used or where he stashed it when he threw his illegal pitch. He knew if he told a teammate about his secret and that person was traded, the word would be all over the league.

Unfortunately, I was hitless in my next ten at bats after that doubleheader. I lived in constant fear that at any moment I was going to be sent back to the minors. But six days after my first start, I had a home run, a double, and a single against the Dodgers, with my dinger coming off Drysdale. Then on Memorial Day my family came to see me play in the big leagues for the first time. It was a doubleheader in Philadelphia. My mother, Rae, an uncle, an aunt, and my girlfriend at the time, Joan Zock from New Jersey, came to see me at Shibe Park. I had another good day, with four hits in the doubleheader.

Another time at Shibe Park that year, Johnny Parascandola came down to watch me play. It was another doubleheader. I didn't play the second game, so I watched from the bullpen. I invited Johnny to come watch with me. In the back of the visiting team's bullpen, in a small storage area where the ground crew kept the bases and equipment, there was a door that opened to the street. I told Johnny to meet me there, and I let him in. Rumor had it that some players would duck out that door during games, sit at a bar in uniform, and drink a beer while watching the game on television. I do know that the visiting bullpen used to be the home team's bullpen. But the Phillies' front office switched bullpens after they found out their players were smuggling women through that door and into the bullpen.

Though many of my friends and family watched me play that year, Sister Marguerite was not allowed to leave the convent. That really bothered me. I wanted everyone in my family to come see me. I wrote a letter on Braves stationery to Cardinal Spellman, the archbishop of New York, asking that he contact the Mother Vicar and allow my sister to come to the ballpark. But they refused to excuse her. The Mother Vicar told her, "Just as you have rules in baseball, so we have rules in the convent." My letter, though, did convince them to allow Sister Marguerite to watch my games on television. The rest of the convent would be at church or a novena or something, and the Mother Vicar would tell her, "Your brother is on. You can stay and watch."

One of the first times I remember Sister Marguerite coming to watch me play was at a doubleheader at Shea Stadium in New York against the Mets on Mother's Day in 1965. She had been assigned to a convent in Connecticut, and her Mother there was much more lenient than before. My mom was at the game too. Before the first game Sister Marguerite gave me a St. Joseph's medal. I pinned it to the inside of the left sleeve of my uniform shirt. Sure enough, I hit a home run and a single. In the second game I popped out my first time up. I looked for the medal and it wasn't there. Suddenly I realized that between games I had changed shirts. I sent the batboy into the clubhouse for the medal and pinned it on the new shirt. I promptly banged out four straight hits, including two more home runs. On each one of my homers I waved to my mother and family in the stands as I ran between second and third base. They stood up and waved back. After the game, instead of traveling with the club to Pittsburgh, I went back to Brooklyn and spent the night at home. When I caught up with the club the next day, I read in the newspapers that

the Mets had tried to obtain me from the Braves—
for half a million dollars. Nothing ever came of it,
except that it was great for my ego.

My early success in my rookie season put me at
ease right away. I wasn't intimidated facing great
pitchers like Drysdale and Koufax—not that the
National League pitchers didn't try to shake me. I
remember facing the Giants for the first time. Jack
Sanford threw his first pitch right at my head. I had
never met the guy before in my life. The game was
different then. At that time they were going to see
how you responded. You were being tested. If they
found out you were afraid, you might as well have
gone home. My thinking—and I felt this way
throughout my career—was that I'd rather get hurt
than be embarrassed. That was the way the game
was played; there was an unwritten but understood
code about throwing at hitters, a code that has disappeared partly because the union and frequent
player movement have diluted the adversarial na-
ture of the game. Players seem too friendly with
their opponents now. I especially hate to see pitchers laughing it up with opponents before games.
They should have an air of mystery about them
when they're facing a hitter.

Those Braves of the early 1960s, the team I grew
up with, were a bunch of rough, tough, hard-bitten
veterans. It was a team with swagger. It was easy for
me to fit in there because I knew most of those
guys. If I had to start out cold with another group
of guys, it would have been a lot harder on me.

Frank also had prepared me for the big leagues by teaching me how to be a professional. For instance, he taught me at an early age that you never touch anybody else's equipment. If I saw Crandall's shin guards with his number on them, I wouldn't touch them. But if his number was crossed out, then I could use them. Knowing how to act made it easier for me to be accepted as a rookie. Spahn and Burdette were especially helpful to me. They were like older brothers. They used to take me to the movies with them in the afternoon and to restaurants at night. Dressen, however, wasn't too hot about me striking up a friendship with them. "Don't hang around Spahn and Burdette," he'd say. "They're like the Katzenjammer Kids."

Spahn and Burdette used to make Dressen's life miserable. Dressen liked to be a disciplinarian, always making sure we made curfew, for instance, which was a big deal in those days. In Chicago, where we always played day games, Dressen would give a baseball to the hotel elevator operator, who came on duty at midnight, and tell him to get every player to autograph it. That way Dressen knew who was late getting in. Guys like Spahn and Burdette, though, caught on to the trick and started signing wrong names on the ball. Spahn and Burdette were also the kind of guys who were always the last ones on the bus. One time Dressen got so fed up with them that he flat-out left them at the airport. Just when they got to the door of the bus, Dressen made the driver close the door and take off without them. Another time Dressen was hiding in the bushes of the Ambassador Hotel in Los Angeles, spying on the players as we would come and go from our cabanas around the main lawn in front. While Dressen was in the bushes keeping an eye on us, Burdette tossed a firecracker in there, scaring the hell out of him.

Dressen always was keeping tabs on us. One day in Pittsburgh he sent a house detective to check on Eddie Mathews and Bob Buhl, a pitcher who had arms like a blacksmith. Neither one of those guys had gone out that night, but Dressen didn't know that. He thought they were still out carousing somewhere. So the house detective knocked on the door to their hotel room. I happened to be in the room across the hall. All of a sudden I heard some yelling and screaming. I ran to my door and peeked out. There was Buhl holding this guy up by his collar with one hand—the detective's feet were dangling about a foot off the ground—and Mathews was standing right over Buhl's shoulder yelling, "Don't you ever pull this shit again, or else we'll knock the crap out of you!"

Mathews was the embodiment of those Braves teams. He was a man's man, a guy who needed a shave every time you saw him, who played the game hard, and who worked to make himself a better player. Eddie had started his career as a bad defensive player but became a pretty good one through sheer hard work—much the way Wade Boggs, my third baseman with the Yankees, worked hard to become a gold glove defensive player. Mathews was one of my idols growing up, and so it was a real thrill to have him as my teammate.

Hank Aaron was one of the quietest players on the team. He would dress immediately after games and go home, just slide out of there without anyone noticing. That was unusual, because in those days players hung out together in the clubhouse after games. I don't know why, but players scatter from the clubhouse much more quickly today. But I never saw Hank off the field. Of course, I realize now that when I played, black players were careful about not going places where they would be embarrassed. There were still many public places where they were not welcome. Hank was a quiet guy anyway, and I think that's why he never got the recognition he truly deserved. I know later in his career he resented not getting proper credit for his extraordinary skills and career. Willie Mays would get much more attention, mostly because he had a much flashier style and played in New York. But Henry was a better hitter than Willie; he had fewer holes. Willie had a knack for rising to the occasion, but Henry would do everything to win a game, including stealing bases when he had to. Willie played center field, a more glamorous position, while Henry played right field. Willie would sometimes fire the baseball to the catcher on the fly, while Henry would always throw the textbook one-hopper to the catcher or hit the cutoff man. That was Hank's style. He didn't call a lot of attention to himself.

I didn't dream at the time, in the early 1960s, that Henry would become baseball's all-time home run king. He wasn't a home run hitter. While Willie would hit those long high flies with his big hard swing, Henry would just smash line drives all over the field with those quick strong wrists of his. Believe me, no one better appreciates his amazing hitting talents than me—I hit behind him in the batting order for eight years. I used to stand there on deck and watch him just devour pitchers, especially young ones. They'd get two strikes on him and figure they could waste a fastball inside and then go away with something off speed—except they'd never get to that second part of their plan. Henry would just eat up fastballs. Never in my life have I seen a better fastball hitter than Henry Aaron.

The one guy who Henry could not hit was Curt Simmons of the St. Louis Cardinals. Simmons once said, "Sneaking a fastball past Henry Aaron is like trying to sneak the sun past a rooster." So Simmons would throw Henry one big, slow sloppy curveball after another, and Henry never hit them. Henry would manage some measly twelve-foot pop-up and have to laugh himself at how easily Simmons could get him out. Then one day in September 1965 Henry decided he'd run up in the batter's box to try to hit that big slow hook before it even reached the plate. He tried it his next to last time up and popped out to shortstop Dal Maxvill. The home plate umpire, Chris Pelokoudas, said to Tim Mc-Carver, who was catching at the time for the Cardinals, "If Maxie drops that ball, I'd have to call him out." In the ninth inning, with the Cardinals ahead by a run, Aaron tried the same thing. This time he blasted the damned pitch on the right-field roof. As soon as Henry made contact, though, Pelokoudas yelled, "You're out!" Well, just about our entire ballclub went nuts. Pelokoudas wound up ejecting several of our guys. I was on deck but managed to stay in the game with a more restrained argument. I asked Pelokoudas, "Would you have made that call if a hitter of lesser stature was up?" He always called his games by the book. It seemed to me that Pelokoudas delighted in making that call. If he hadn't, the magical number atop the all-time home run list would be 756, not 755.

I had three managers in my first three seasons in the big leagues: Dressen, the J. Edgar Hoover of managers; Birdie Tebbetts, who replaced Dressen midway through the 1961 season; and Bobby Bragan, who actually lasted three and a half years before he too was fired. I had a tough time playing for the Braves in 1962. Crandall was back playing, and I became a cold weather catcher. If Tebbetts thought it was too cold to risk Crandall's cranky shoulder, he'd start me instead. I hit .282 that year with only 220 at bats, about half as many as the previous season. Every day when I came to the park, I didn't know if I'd be playing or not. I hated that.

But I'll always remember that Birdie Tebbetts used to say something about himself that applies to me as a manager now: He was easier to get along with when his team was losing than when it was winning. As long as players are giving you their best effort when they're losing, what can you do? If you start yelling and screaming at them, you'll only make them more uptight. I've always felt more compassion for players when my teams were losing. But if we were making mistakes while we were winning, it would aggravate me, because over the long haul you're not going to get away with mental mistakes. Don Zimmer, my bench coach with the Yankees, found out that I'm more of a stickler when we're winning. Somebody would miss a sign or a cutoff man, and I'd get angry in the dugout. Zim would say, "Relax, what are you getting excited about?" That's what was so great about having him around. He gave me energy when I needed it and calm when I needed that.

By 1963 I had wrested the starting catching job away from Crandall. That was the year I made the all-star team for the first of five straight seasons, a year I hit .293 with 14 home runs. My career was taking off, and the Braves knew it. They traded Crandall to San Francisco after the 1963 season. The job was mine, though I'll always be grateful to Crandall for being a true professional and being so quick to help me during my first few years in the big leagues. Beginning with that difficult 1962 season, my home run total improved four straight years, from five to 14 to 20 to 27 to 36. In 1965, only my sixth year of catching, I won a Gold Glove as the finest defensive catcher in the National League. My star was shining—so brightly, in fact, that it even blinded some people. In 1964 my manager at the time, Bobby Bragan, said, "There is no doubt in my mind that he will become one of the truly great players of baseball. I wouldn't trade him for anybody you could name, and that includes Willie Mays, Sandy Koufax, and all the rest."

I had become one of the elite players in the game. But the eight seasons I played with the Braves—five in Milwaukee and three in Atlanta— were far from gratifying. Not only did we not win anything over those years, but we never even managed to play our way into a pennant race. Once again my timing was terrible. Before I arrived in 1960, Milwaukee very nearly had won four straight pennants. It finished a close second in 1956 (losing out to the Dodgers on the last day of the season), finished first in 1957 and 1958, and lost a best-of-three playoff to the Dodgers in 1959 after the two clubs finished the regular season tied. (The Braves lost both playoff games by one run.) Frank was lucky enough to play on all of those great Milwaukee teams. My years with the Braves included not a whiff of such greatness. We were never terrible but almost always barely a notch above mediocre. From 1960 through 1968 my Braves teams won between 81 and 88 games every year but one, 1967, when we managed only 77 wins.

We were a club that could pound the ball as well as anyone. In 1965 we set a National League record with six players hitting at least twenty home runs—and finished fifth. Our problem was that we couldn't hold down the other teams. We never had enough pitching. I joined the Braves just as the golden years of pitchers—Spahn, Burdette, and Buhl—were running out. The pitchers who followed them, such as Tony Cloninger, Hank Fischer, Wade Blasingame, and Denny Lemaster, never developed into the same kind of consistent winners.

I hungered for more than just playing decent baseball. I wanted desperately to reach my dream of playing in the World Series. Through Frank I had seen what it was like to play for a winner. And in 1960, when I was a wide-eyed kid in the big leagues for the first time, I saw the excitement in Pittsburgh as the Pirates prepared for the World Series. We played a series there at the end of the year that meant nothing as far as the standings were concerned. The Pirates had already clinched the pennant. But I could feel the electricity in the air. It was invigorating. It was what I wanted. It reminded me of being in the clubhouse in 1957 in Milwaukee with Frank. For the next thirty-five years I hated to watch the celebrations after the World Series or championship football or basketball games ended. It was like watching somebody else eat a hot fudge sundae. I wanted one too.

CHAPTER 5
Growing Up Again

I LOVED THE MAJOR LEAGUE LIFE—THE hotels, the travel, the restaurants, the nightlife, and all the trappings that come with being recognized wherever you go. People considered ballplayers heroes in those days, not as millionaire celebrities as they do now. I was earning $17,500, a decent amount of money for 1963. I was young, and I was single. But not for long. In the early 1960s Frank and I used to go to Miami every January to begin working out for the season. We'd stay at a motel, work out with some other big league players at Flamingo Park, go to the racetrack, and then hit the nightclubs, including the Playboy Club in Miami. One night, in January 1963, I met a twenty-one-year-old Playboy bunny named Jackie. I married her nine months later.

Looking back, I was much too immature and

irresponsible at the time to get married. I'm embarrassed to think of how I acted then. I didn't listen to my family's constant warnings that I wasn't ready to get married. I felt I had reached a level of independence from my family where I didn't need to listen to them. The first time I brought my fiancée to meet Sister Marguerite, we went to her convent on Long Island. Sitting next to me in the company of a nun, my sister, Jackie started stroking my thigh with her hand. I did nothing to stop her. Sister Marguerite's eyes grew wide as they lowered to watch what was happening. She knew right then we had no business being married.

The spring after I met Jackie was the first time the Braves trained in West Palm Beach after all those years on the west coast of Florida. I got to see Jackie often. We rushed through our engagement, and then, on October 21, 1963, we were married without anyone in my family in attendance. I didn't bother inviting them because I knew they all disapproved of the marriage. I'm sure I hurt them very much, especially my mother. It didn't take very long for us to find out our marriage wasn't working. It seemed like we were talking about a divorce almost immediately. And then, two months after we were married, Jackie became pregnant. We put our divorce plans on hold until after the baby was born.

We never really set up a traditional home but moved from one apartment to another. It was a very disjointed relationship. I can never say, though, that my first marriage was a big mistake or that I regret it. That's because out of that marriage my son Michael was born. He's always been the kind of son that makes a father proud, even if this father may not have devoted as much time as he should have to raising him. I was having too much fun in those days. I was like a kid in a candy store, thinking I should have anything that I wanted without attaching any responsibility to it. Sadly, sometimes I applied that attitude to my family.

Because of my experiences at that age, I have a keen understanding of how and why young players get swept away with themselves when they get to the big leagues. Two of my players with the Yankees, Dwight Gooden and Darryl Strawberry, are prime examples of that. I'm patient with the attitude of some young players because I was a rebel myself. But there's a big difference between being selfish off the field and being selfish on the field. I'm very proud to have been an unselfish player throughout my career. I have little tolerance for a player who puts his personal goals ahead of winning.

After the 1964 season ended, and seven weeks after Michael was born, Jackie and I started divorce proceedings. I ended up retaining custody of Michael, who basically was raised by my mother and Rae, until my mother's death, when Sister Marguerite got permission from her superiors to live at home with them in Brooklyn. He grew up in Frank's and my bedroom at our house on Avenue T.

At the age of twenty-three, after batting .293 in

1963, I held out of Milwaukee's training camp because of a salary dispute. I stayed out of camp for three weeks until they came up with a number I liked: $28,000. And then I went out and had a breakthrough season in 1964. I batted .321, with 20 home runs and 109 runs batted in. The Braves rewarded me with a raise to $39,500.

It was in that 1964 season that the Braves announced plans to move the franchise to Atlanta. The people of Milwaukee tried to muster enough support to keep the team there. We drew almost one million people that season while finishing in fifth place, only five games behind the league champion Cardinals in a tightly packed race. Still, that was not an overwhelming show of support for a franchise that had drawn more than twice that many fans (2.2 million) only seven years earlier. We were bound for Atlanta. The city of Milwaukee, though, kept us there for one more season by obtaining a restraining order in court to postpone the move. It was a terrible decision because it created a lame duck status for us. In 1965 we drew only 555,584 fans. Every night at County Stadium, it was like playing in front of your closest friends.

I didn't shed a single tear about leaving Milwaukee, even though I had great memories of the place during the years my brother Frank and I were there. I was at a selfish stage in my life where I wanted a more exciting city. Milwaukee had some nice restaurants and would have been fine if I were older, but it had very little nightlife. I couldn't wait to get to Atlanta and Peachtree Street, where all the bars and clubs were. I remembered visiting the city in 1954 when Frank played there in the minor leagues. It was a dynamic, vibrant town. I recalled a minor league all-star game there in 1954 that drew so many people that they put the overflow part of the crowd in the outfield and rigged up a rope fence in front of them. I knew Atlanta would be more excited about having a baseball team than Milwaukee.

I thought I was hot stuff then. In 1965, in discussing my $39,500 salary with a reporter, I joked that "I don't keep much of it anyway. Between taxes and my love for clothes, it all goes." That wasn't far from the truth, though I was also great at picking up tabs at restaurants and bars. I owned eight suits at that time, for which I paid about $150 each—a princely sum in those days. I bought them from Gene Oliver, one of my Braves teammates who worked in the off-season at a Rock Island, Illinois, clothing shop. I also bragged to the reporter that I owned about forty-five shirts, fifty ties, and seven pairs of shoes. I still enjoy nice clothes and shopping for them.

I became so full of myself that around that time Frank scolded me for forgetting about Mom. "Damn it, Joe," he said to me on the telephone one day. "You know she was your mother before you became a big leaguer, and she doesn't love you because you're in the big leagues. She loves you as a person, and you've got to treat her accordingly." I can't say the message hit home immediately. I spent too much of those years in the mid-1960s acting like a jerk. Frank, in fact, became so ashamed of my irresponsibility that he stopped talking to me for a year or so.

Atlanta suited me fine in every way. In addition to christening the ballpark there with its first home run, I went on to hit thirty-six home runs that season, a record for a Braves catcher that still stands. Balls fly out of Atlanta County Stadium because of the warm air and lack of troublesome winds. It got to the point where the ballpark was referred to as "the Launching Pad." I also batted .315, knocked in 101 runs, and established myself as one of the true clubhouse cutups. One day I flopped around the clubhouse wearing a complete outfit of scuba gear that belonged to Felipe Alou, my teammate. My defense, though, worsened. My work habits behind the plate were getting sloppy. After winning a Gold Glove the previous season, I made 11 errors and was charged with 13 passed balls in 1965. My manager, Billy Hitchcock, told me after the season that I needed to lose weight; I probably weighed about 220 pounds at the time. "I'd hate to see Torre remembered as simply a good hitting catcher," Hitchcock told the press, "because he has the talent—and has shown it—to be one of the best defensive catchers around. He could wind up as the greatest all-round catcher of all time."

I did briefly lose a little weight, with the help of three weeks of military life and cutting back on the food on a goodwill baseball tour of Vietnam after the 1966 season. After a sendoff from President Johnson in Washington, I traveled there with five others: Mel Allen, Brooks Robinson, Harmon Killebrew, Hank Aaron, and Stan Musial. In other words, everyone in our party except me wound up in the Hall of Fame. In January 1997 I failed on my fifteenth and final try to be voted into the Hall of Fame by the baseball writers. If only I had managed seventeen more hits while I was playing—just one extra hit each season—I would have finished with a lifetime .300 batting average instead of .297. That would have improved my candidacy, though I never had the great power numbers or postseason exposure that catches voters' attention. I am, however, a proud member of the Parade Grounds Hall of Fame and the Italian American Hall of Fame.

My trip to Vietnam had its scary moments, but I guess it helped me that I still was young and a little wild at the time. I didn't have enough sense to be afraid. We spent one afternoon in Da Nang having lunch at the home of a General Walt. The next day, after we had left, it was mortared. The planes we traveled in would get fired at by the Vietcong, though not enough to cause serious damage. I did, however, see many bullet holes in the wings. Because that was a strange war where there were no lines drawn, it was difficult to tell who was the enemy. But whenever we were flying, we could tell the Vietcong from the Vietnamese: the Vietcong were the ones diving for cover into the rice paddies.

Most of our time during the day was spent shaking hands and talking baseball with the troops. But one night they asked Stan Musial and me to visit a small unit in a cemetery. They gave us both pistols. We drove in a jeep with the headlights off for camouflage; the driver had to point a flashlight straight down the narrow pathway to see where we were going. Stan was sitting in the front, afraid to say a word. He didn't like it one bit. I sat in the back. As I said, I was young and stupid, and I was having a good time on the trip being with these great baseball players. It was like an extension of the season for me. When we got to the place where the unit was stationed, we discovered about twenty troops bunkered in a tiny hut made out of ammunition boxes. Stan decided he was going to stay in the jeep. I joined the unit and said hello to the guys. Then at nine o'clock the unit started harassment fire, in which they expel rounds just so the Vietcong wouldn't get comfortable. They happened to be firing right over the top of Stan and the jeep. He couldn't wait to get the hell out of there.

I'll always remember how happy the troops were to see us. Those guys were great and, no matter what their condition, loved talking baseball with us. I recall visiting this one soldier and staring at his helmet. It had one hole in the front and another on the side. A bullet had gone through the front, grazed his head, and gone out the side. He was lucky. I left with enormous respect for those fighting men. And they made me feel lucky too. As a ballplayer, I was required only to join the reserves. I was fortunate not to be in harm's way like them.

The next season, 1967, had to be the height of my irresponsibility. We had an awful team that year, the first losing season for the Braves since 1952. We finished in seventh place, twenty-four and a half games out of first place, but we led the league in drinking and hospitality. That was also the year Clete Boyer and Bob Uecker joined the Braves and became my partners in crime. Boyer and I bought a bar in Atlanta called Pig Alley. Players from other clubs used to come to our place to drink, and we never charged them anything. It was a hell of a place. I don't know how we did it, but I think we ended up losing only about five dollars apiece on that investment. Pig Alley was one of the big reasons why the newspapers used to call that Braves team "the playboys of Peachtree."

On June 6, 1967, the Braves made a trade with the Phillies to get my buddy Uecker. Uke has made a second career for himself by making fun of his baseball abilities, but he was a good defensive catcher with a strong arm who was particularly adept at catching knuckleball pitchers. Atlanta figured he would be perfect for Phil Niekro, our ace knuckleballer. That was fine with me. I knew how difficult it was to catch that pitch. I had a standard line when people asked me how to catch the knuckler: "Use a big glove and a pair of rosary beads." On the first day Uke joined our team, I laid out a white carpet of towels from the door to his locker, where I hung a sign: "Thank You Very Much. God Bless You. And Lots of Luck. Your Buddy, Phil Niekro."

I was so happy to see Uke again that I invited him to be my roommate in Atlanta. We stayed in an apartment complex that loosely was arranged in two sections, one for families and one for singles. Somehow I was in the family section when Uecker joined me. We threw great loud parties in that place, always inviting players from visiting teams to drop in. Unfortunately, drinking was an accepted and sometimes encouraged form of behavior around baseball in those days. I'm glad we've come a long way since then.

The people who ran that apartment complex finally got so fed up with our parties that they kicked us out into the singles section. The apartments there had the exact same floor plan as the ones on the family side, only they were reversed—like a mirror image. On our first night after moving to the new apartment, Uke and I went out and partied long and hard. I made it home first. A while later I heard Uke come through the door. Then I heard him stumbling down the hallway, bouncing off the walls in the dark. He reached for the door of what he thought was the bathroom, took a step inside, and threw up. When we awoke, we found out that Uke actually had thrown up in a closet; he was accustomed to the old apartment and wasn't sober enough to remember the reversed floor plan.

Uke wound up catching a lot after joining us

because I had a strained ligament in my ankle. I wore a cast for a while and couldn't play. That happened to be during the middle of the summer, while we had a grueling stretch of doubleheaders. Uke used to kid with me every day about my injury. "How long are you going to nurse that thing?" he'd say. "What's the big deal about a cast? You can play with a cast. Just tape it up and get out there. I'm wasting away here. My hat size has already shrunk from a seven and a quarter to a five while you're milking that injury. I figure the more I play, the closer I am to going back to the minors."

One day during that 1967 season, we were taking batting practice before a game against the New York Mets at Shea Stadium when I noticed a great-looking blonde sitting in the stands. A New York photographer I knew, Louie Requena, came up to me and asked if he could take a picture of me.

"Sure," I told him, "on one condition."

"What's that?" Louie said.

I pointed to the woman. "If you get her phone number for me, I'll let you take the picture."

"Get out of here; you're too ugly," he said.

"No picture then," I replied.

Louie reluctantly walked over to the railing and explained to the woman that I would like her phone number. She agreed to give it to him. I called her later, and we arranged to see each other the next time I came to New York with the Braves. Six months after that, in January 1968, Dani and I were married in the house of friends of mine, Charlie and Mary Helen Luke from Atlanta. Again, I didn't bother inviting anyone from my family because I knew they approved of this whirlwind courtship about as much as my first one.

My luck with marriage didn't get any better, and my baseball career hit some bumps too. Early in that 1968 season, on April 18, we were facing the Cubs in Atlanta, and I was batting against a small right-handed relief pitcher named Chuck Hartenstein. The count was one ball and two strikes. Hank Aaron was on first base with two outs. I knew Henry had a habit of stealing when the count worked against the hitter. As Hartenstein swung his arm back to deliver the ball, I took a peek at Henry to see if he was going to run. I saw him take off. And when I refocused my vision to pick up the ball coming out of Hartenstein's hand, I couldn't find it. I never saw it. It smashed against my cheek. It split my palate, broke my cheek and my nose. It's a wonder I didn't lose any teeth. My teammates had to carry me off the field and into the clubhouse. I was in shock. The trainer held a finger up and asked me to follow it, but I couldn't. I couldn't see. They took me to a hospital where I spent the next three or four days. It took almost that long for the bleeding in my nose to stop.

Although there was no permanent damage, I couldn't play for five or six weeks. I watched the games from the press box. It wasn't like now, where guys on the disabled list stay in uniform and watch games from the bench. The way we do it now is much better because it keeps players more involved in what's happening with the club. After one of those games while I was hurt, I went out to dinner with a friend of mine from Pittsburgh, Joel Aranson, who was in Atlanta on business. I had my usual share of cocktails and wine with the meal. Driving home in the early morning hours, I decided to straighten out some of the curves on Peachtree Street. All of a sudden I saw police lights in my rearview mirror. I pulled over, and the officer asked if I had been drinking. "Yeah," I said. "I had some wine." He took my license and recognized me. Unlike Frank's run-in with the law after the 1958 World Series, I wasn't let off the hook. He put me in the paddy wagon and hauled me back to the station—but not before stopping twice to have me sign autographs for his friends. They arrested me for driving under the influence. I called up a friend of mine who was a policeman, Buddy Whalen, and told him I was in jail. He thought I was kidding, but then he arranged for me to be released on my own recognizance.

"Don't worry," he said. "Nobody's going to know about this."

Later that day, as I got a ride back to the station to pick up my car, news of my drunk driving arrest was on the radio about every fifteen minutes. The fans got on me pretty good about that. I blamed the cop for not letting me go; I hadn't been driving that fast anyway. But looking back, I realize I was so spoiled that I easily placed blame on other people but never on myself. I wish I had had the same kind of mature attitude that John Wetteland had with the Yankees in 1996. He was unhappy that the front office fought him during the year over a clause in his contract that permitted him to be a free agent after the season. He also was angry that they discouraged him from Rollerblading around the stadium, one of his favorite pastimes. But John never let that affect him. He went about his business like a professional and was one of the best closers in baseball last season.

We managed to play .500 ball that 1968 season, a year noteworthy in retrospect only because our team featured three future managers (myself, Alou, and Dusty Baker) and a sixty-two-year-old pitcher, Satchel Paige. Actually, Bill Bartholomay, the Braves' president, signed Satchel as a trainer because he heard that Satchel was short the necessary service time to qualify for a pension. Satchel wasn't on the active roster, but he would put a uniform on and be on the field before games. In the clubhouse he'd sit in his chair and tell stories, and we'd gather around him, like a family clustered around the pot-bellied stove. He told us how his control had been so good that he could throw a baseball over a resin bag. He told us about the great players of the Negro League, like Cool Papa Bell, who he said was so fast, he could turn out the light and be in bed before the room got dark. And he told us he personally didn't believe in running. "You might step in a hole," he explained.

I played in only 115 games in 1968 because of getting hit in the face with the pitch. I batted .271, a career low at that point, with 10 home runs and 55 runs batted in. I had a hard time getting my confidence back after being beaned. It wasn't until the next year that I convinced myself I had to either get over it or quit. Paul Richards, the Braves' general manager, wanted to cut my salary from $65,000 to $52,000—the maximum twenty percent pay cut allowed. I guess Richards figured it was my fault that my face got in the way of a baseball and I should pay for it. I think he also disliked me because I served as our team's player representative to the union, which was gaining increased strength under the strong and wise leadership of Marvin Miller. Richards hated Marvin intensely.

What bothered me even more than the proposed pay cut was that Richards made statements in the press that I hadn't done very much for the club over the previous two seasons and that as far as he was concerned I could hold out until Thanksgiving. I decided there was no way I was signing anything unless Richards offered me a public apology. I was a spring training holdout again. It wasn't just about money anymore. I knew I had to take a stand to regain the respect of my teammates. I could not allow myself to be publicly insulted like that and just walk into the clubhouse as if nothing had happened. Besides, it wasn't as if I still was a young player who needed to sign quickly because I needed the money. Those days were over for me. I was working in the off-season selling municipal bonds for a firm called Valeriano & Craig on Wall Street. A lot of players took off-season jobs in those days. Warren Spahn, for instance, worked on his cattle ranch. Besides, the way I was spending money, I needed a second job. Valeriano & Craig paid me $1,000 a month over the calendar year. The firm told me I could keep working for them as long as I wanted. They even gave me my own business cards.

Bill Bartholomay called me up at my home in New Jersey and said, "There must be some way we can work this out between you and Paul Richards. Why don't you come down to Florida, and you two guys can talk about it? He's ready to make you another offer, but it's not going to be a raise."

"I'll come down," I said, "on one condition: You buy me a round-trip ticket."

"Fine," Bartholomay said. "We'll see you in West Palm Beach."

I flew down the next day or so. I figured Richards would offer me the same salary I had the year before. I walked into Richards's office at the ballpark in West Palm Beach, where the Braves trained.

"Well, what did you want to see me about?" I said to Richards.

"I didn't want to see you," he said.

"Bill Bartholomay said you were ready to make another offer," I said.

"The same deal stands—not one cent different," Richards said.

"What about an apology for what you said about me?"

"I don't see the need for an apology. I don't consider those remarks I made personal. This is a business."

"I'm sorry, but I consider them very personal to me."

Then I reached into my wallet for one of my Valeriano & Craig business cards. I threw it on Richards's desk. "Well," I said, "if you ever need me, here's how to reach me."

Richards took my card and threw it in a trash can. And that was it. I walked out. I knew my ten years of service to the Braves organization were over.

The New York papers were full of rumors about me being traded to the Mets. I thought I wanted to go—playing at home and all that—but deep down I wasn't sure. Sometimes playing at home can be distracting, what with all the ticket requests and the pressure to do well in front of family and friends.

I later found out that Richards did try to trade me to the Mets. He was prepared to trade Bob Aspromonte and me in exchange for pitcher Nolan Ryan, catcher J. C. Martin, first baseman Ed Kranepool, and third baseman/outfielder Amos Otis. The Mets agreed on the entire package except Otis. Richards knew Otis was untouchable. The Mets countered by saying they would replace Otis in the deal with infielder Bobby Heise. Richards turned them down.

Then on St. Patrick's Day, 1969, Richards traded me to the St. Louis Cardinals for first baseman Orlando Cepeda, a former most valuable player who had been a colorful, popular figure in St. Louis. The Cardinals had won the two previous National League pennants and had been the 1967 world champions. I told my mother the news, and she said, "Now go to church and thank God." When Bing Devine, the Cardinals' general manager, called me up with news of the trade, we negotiated a contract in about one minute over the phone. Bing asked me what I wanted. I told him I wanted the same contract I had with Atlanta the previous year: $65,000 and the use of a car. He told me the Cardinals did not include the use of free cars in their contracts, but that he'd give me $70,000. I took it. Not quite the same process that goes on today. Bing was such a classy guy that when I flew to Florida to join the Cardinals in St. Petersburg, he was at the airport to greet me.

That was the first season of divisional play, and I remember talking in spring training about how the West Division teams would be fighting it out for the right to play against us in the playoffs. I should have known better. My timing, as usual, was awful. After two straight World Series appearances, the Cardinals slipped to fourth place in the East Division as soon as I got there. We finished 87–75, thirteen games out of first place.

And what about my former club, the Braves?
They won the West Division, of course. And who
did they play in the National League Championship
Series? The Mets, naturally. The team that I *wasn't*
traded to. I started to think I was the black cloud,
and so did some of my more humorous Cardinal
teammates. Bob Gibson used to say to me, "You
know, we used to win before you got here." When
the Mets clinched their East Division title that
year, they did so by beating us at Shea Stadium.
And who took care of the final outs by grounding
into a double play? Yours truly. The Mets went on
to win the World Series, with the series MVP award
going to Donn Clendenon, the first baseman whom
the Mets had acquired after failing to get me. If
that wasn't enough, Dani insisted that we go to
Shea Stadium to watch the World Series in person. I
had to go there and watch her root for the Mets.
Now that was torture. I saw Game Four, the one in
which Ron Swoboda made that diving catch in
right field. That definitely was not the way I
wanted to get to the World Series.

I had a good year for the Cardinals in 1969—
knocking in 101 runs and batting .289 while playing mostly first base because Tim McCarver still
was the regular catcher in St. Louis. I felt a lot of
pressure trying to replace Cepeda but found myself
surrounded by a great bunch of teammates. The
Cardinals were coming off two straight pennants.
They knew how to win, and they had this professional, cool personality that contrasted with the

rough-and-tough style of the Braves teams I had known. Red Schoendienst was the perfect manager for those Cardinals. As a manager, sometimes you assume a lot—that your players know what they are supposed to do and that they understand your moves. Red was able to take that approach because he had such a smart seasoned bunch. And luckily, so did I with the Yankees. It was the first year that kind of approach worked for me. The Yankees' professionalism really made me think back to those classy Cardinal teams.

The first guy who welcomed me to the team was Bob Gibson. The team was on a trip when I joined them in spring training, and right away Gibson made a joke of trying to get me to steal McCarver's number, 15, which had been my number with the Braves. He took the number 15 that hung above McCarver's locker and tacked it up over mine. (The Cardinals gave me number 9, which I thought was great because it had belonged to Roger Maris, a player I much admired.) Like most people, I was a little intimidated by Gibson at first. He was notorious for knocking down hitters and never talking to opponents. The first time I met him was actually at the 1965 all-star game. Gibby was pitching, and I was catching. He worked ahead of Tony Oliva, the leadoff hitter, no balls and two strikes. I knew Gibson hated catchers coming out to the mound under any circumstance; he figured he knew more about pitching than they did. But I knew that Oliva liked to hit pitches down and in, and I wanted to make certain Gibby knew that.

"This guy's a good hitter who likes the ball down and in," I told Gibson. "Let's keep it up and in." He basically just snarled at me in response.

Oliva hit the first pitch Gibson threw—it was down and in—for a double. It turned out to be harmless because an obviously perturbed Gibby retired the next three batters, striking out Joe Pepitone, on three blazing, high fastballs. Afterward I happened to be in the shower room with Gibson. We were standing under adjacent nozzles. "Nice game," I said. Gibby never even turned his head to acknowledge me. I think I detected a grunt out of him—that was it. He wouldn't talk to me. I had no idea at the time that Gibby would turn out to be one of my very best friends in life—and not just among the baseball people I know. We're so close that he's become like another brother to me. Gibby is also the one guy I'd pick for my pitcher if I had to win one game. Nobody I know has ever been better at pitching the big game. Maybe a couple of guys could be his equal at it, but no one's been better.

I didn't become close with McCarver right away. In fact, I remember there was some unspoken tension between us my first year in St. Louis. We had been rivals as catchers—always in a duel, for instance, at balloting time for the all-star game—and now we were on the same club, even though the Cardinals got me to play first base. After the 1969 season St. Louis traded Timmy to Philadelphia, in the same deal that prompted Curt Flood to challenge baseball's reserve clause. I got a lot closer to Timmy when he returned to the Cardinals in 1974. We had a lot in common: a love of food, wine, and the nuances of baseball, to begin with.

Timmy and I talked a lot about managing in those days. We actually kicked around the idea of some day becoming comanagers of a team. During that 1969 season Timmy, Gibson, Dal Maxvill, and myself formed what we called "the Dinner Club." Every time we played a day game on the road, we'd get together for dinner. We'd spend most of the night talking about the strategies and intricacies of baseball. On any given night, there would be six to nine players joining us. I've never seen such a large group of players consistently going out together.

We used to love to drink expensive wine with good dinners. And we always split the tab equally, whether any one of us ate much or not. In other words, you had to pay for the privilege of eating with us.

Timmy and I were almost always the first ones at the ballpark. One of our coaches, George Kissell, always was there early too. The three of us would spend hours talking about baseball. Looking back on it, that's when I started to get the foundation for my managing career. I learned more baseball from George Kissell than from anyone else in my life. He used to have a great saying: The most important word in the baseball dictionary is *why*. And that's pretty much what Timmy, George, and I would do. We'd constantly ask ourselves why things had happened in games. Sometimes Gibby and Maxie would sit in too. They were very stimulating and enlightening sessions.

With the Cardinals, a team that didn't score runs nearly as readily as the Braves, George showed me how to create runs by stealing bases and moving runners. He taught me that while running to first base, you should run *through* the bag and not *to* it. He taught me that outfielders should reposition themselves according to the count on the hitter, and not just plant themselves in the same spot. And he taught me an unorthodox defense with a runner on third when it's time to bring the infield in: With a right-handed hitter, and with the count in his favor, you leave your third baseman back at normal depth. That puts pressure on the runner and third-base coach in whether to decide to break for home on a ground ball. It's good thinking, and I've used a number of George's defensive inventions throughout my career. But as I found out in Game One of the 1996 World Series, it's not guaranteed to work. I kept my shortstop, Derek Jeter, back at normal depth with runners on second and third, one out, and Chipper Jones batting right-handed. We were down 2–0 in the third inning and wanted to avoid a big Atlanta rally. When my pitcher, Andy Pettitte, worked the count to one ball, two strikes, I brought Jeter in, figuring Jones would have a more defensive swing with the count against him. He promptly grounded a single past Jeter, driving in two runs.

Surrounded by those intelligent, dedicated professionals in St. Louis, I finally began to grow up and mature. Timmy and Maxie, in particular, taught me a lot about being very positive all the time. Maxie would tell me things about myself I didn't know: that I was a team player and a guy who could handle pressure. I thought that until you went to the World Series, you hadn't proved you could handle pressure. That was my mindset.

Steve Carlton was another guy who loved to have fun, talk baseball, and enjoy wine. He was my roommate for a while. He pitched one of the most amazing games I ever saw. In 1969 I was playing first base when Lefty struck out nineteen batters— and lost. Swoboda hit two two-run home runs to beat him, 4–3. The next season, 1970, Carlton had even worse luck and wound up losing nineteen games. One time that year we were playing the Reds in Cincinnati on a Saturday afternoon. Lefty always had trouble with Johnny Bench. He couldn't get Johnny out if it was midnight and no lights were turned on. That day Johnny hit three home runs off Lefty: one to left field, one to center field, and one to right field. After the game Lefty and I commiserated over dinner and a little wine. I guess we had more than a little wine. When we got back to our hotel suite, I think we broke every stick of furniture in the room. When we awoke in the morning and realized what we had done, we tried to glue everything back together. It wasn't very well-made stuff. We bought glue and delicately put the tables and chairs back together. When we left the suite, we had to make sure we didn't close the door too hard because we were afraid the noise would cause everything to fall apart.

Lefty was a mess that year. He began pitching very defensively. He fell in love with his breaking ball and wouldn't use his fastball. Once in a while I'd ask Red Schoendienst if I could catch Lefty. One time in Los Angeles every single pitch I called was a fastball. He shook me off one time, and it was a two-run home run. Lefty beat the Dodgers 3–2.

In contrast to Lefty, I had a great year in 1970. I finished second in the batting race, with a .325 average, and knocked in a hundred runs. I really felt comfortable in St. Louis. I had somehow come over to the Cardinals with a reputation as a trouble-maker with management. I was there for two years when somebody in the front office told me, "You know what? You're not a troublemaker." I'd tell people, "I had trouble with Paul Richards. That was it." But I did settle down as a more mature person. As a sign of my newfound responsibility, in spring training of that season I finally took off my excess poundage for good. I had played most of my career in the range of 220 to 230 pounds. With McCarver traded and with his heir apparent, Ted Simmons, scheduled to miss the first two months in the service, I knew I'd have to open the season behind the plate. I had to get in better shape. Also, I was a little concerned about turning thirty that season. I knew you had to work harder to stay in shape once you hit that mark. My brother Frank told me about Dr. Stillman's water diet. You drink eighty ounces of water a day and eat a ton of protein—eggs, steaks, things like that. I had a refrigerator full of hard-boiled eggs. Every time you eat a hard-boiled egg and then have two or three glasses of water, it's like swallowing a sponge and filling it up. That's the idea; you're full.

The diet worked. I lost twenty pounds in spring training, dropping from 228 to 208. During the season I actually went all the way down to 195, and my waist shrank so much—to about thirty-two inches—that I briefly had to wear the batboy's pants. The diet also made me aware of everything I put in my mouth. I was the kind of guy who thought nothing of eating candy, soft drinks, banana cream pies, and junk like that. But I really watched what I ate after the diet and learned to reduce my portions. That's the way I am to this day: I love to eat good food—and sometimes the table in front of me will be filled with different dishes—but I enjoy it in small quantities.

Jack Buck, the Cardinals' broadcaster, thought I got too skinny in the early 1970s and had lost some of my power. I didn't think that was true. But I didn't have the heart to tell people the real reason I kept losing weight: I was a nervous wreck because of my family life. Dani and I just were not meant for each other. I couldn't relax in my own home because we weren't communicating well. On top of that, my daughter Tina, who was born in 1968 without a hip socket, seemed always to be in a hospital or seeing specialists. It wasn't until Tina was six years old that she underwent surgery at the Children's Hospital in Toronto, in which Dr. Robert Salter split her pelvis to form a hip out of it. Later on, when I was managing, I'd take the money from the fines I collected from my players over the course of a year and send it to Dr. Salter for his research.

Dani had been married at nineteen to one of the band members of Jay Black and the Americans. She had danced on Broadway a little bit. We were just a bad combination. I'm sure she must have been unhappy too. The atmosphere in our house was chilly. I'll never forget when one of my friends came to visit us, and as he left he whispered to me, "Is it always like this here?" "Yes," I told him. So I poured myself into my work, and as a result I played well, but our marriage suffered even more.

It's sad to say, but 1970 and 1971, when I really kind of shut off my family life and concentrated on my job, turned out to be the two best years of my career. Baseball was mine. It was my accomplishment. Dani couldn't mess with that. Looking back, I was wrong to think that way, but at the time I felt like that was the only way that I could do my job. When Dani brought it to my attention, I tried to change. I admitted I *was* selfish, and that I wasn't very good at being a family man and a ballplayer at the same time. So I tried to change. And this is what happened: I couldn't do either one well. I wasn't very good at home, and I went to the ballpark worrying about that, and so I wasn't very good there either. My career was never the same afterward.

That 1971 season, though, turned out to be my career year, my MVP season. Sadly, my father wasn't alive to see it. In January of that year, my father left for his usual winter getaway. On the very first day he got there, he suffered a stroke and died. He was sixty-eight years old. Frank and I arranged to have the body returned to New York for burial.

George Kissell turned me into a third baseman in spring training in 1971. We'd worked out together every morning from eight-thirty to nine, just doing all kinds of drills. For instance, he'd stand behind me and throw a ball off a concrete wall, and I'd have to react to its bounce and catch it. The more we did it, the closer I moved to the wall, and the closer I moved to the wall, the more my reaction time quickened. On the first day of the drills, George said to me, "Take your stance." He didn't like it—he thought I had my feet spread too wide. He didn't come right out and say it, though. Instead, he asked me, "You know Bob Cousy, the basketball player?"

"Sure," I said.

"If he had the basketball right now in front of you, how would you guard him?"

I immediately shortened up my stance. That's what George wanted to see.

"Why'd you do that?" he said.

"So he can't drive by me to the right and he can't drive by me to the left," I said.

"Good," he said. "Look at your feet. From now on that's where they'll be playing third base."

I learned one of my many lessons from George that day. As a manager, you have to find a way to communicate with people—to correct and suggest things—without having them resent you for it. That's what I try to do: get a message across to the player by getting him to sort of agree with me, rather than scolding and lecturing.

I led the National League third basemen in errors that year, but in time I made myself into a good defensive player and took pride in my glovework, especially since all those who scouted me as a teenager had said I could never play the infield. Of course, I was red hot at the plate all season. I was so consistent, it was scary. My monthly batting averages, starting with April, went like this: .366, .355, .393, .324, .368, and .368. I batted .363 against right-handers and .362 against left-handers.

I was locked in all year. I used to go home and know what pitches I was going to hit off the pitcher the next day. It was weird. I had such a feeling of concentration, of being able to block everything out. And the more hits you get, the more confident you are. The key is your confidence level.

I had a ton of hits to right field that year, even

more than I usually did. My philosophy on hitting was pretty simple: Dare 'em to jam you. For some reason, hitters are embarrassed to get jammed. I think there are a lot more hits on the handle than on the end of the bat. Normally, if you hit the ball on the end of the bat, it means your head is coming off the ball—leaning back and away from it. I like to tell kids and even big league players that the front shoulder is the key to good hitting. You have to keep that shoulder pointed toward the pitcher. Once it opens up away from the ball, your head follows, and it shortens the area of the plate you can cover with your bat. You wind up hitting the ball off the end of the bat. Frank had taught me all about this and more. He always served me as something of a personal hitting coach. Even in 1971, when I was pounding the ball, Frank would talk to me three times a week, reminding me in his usual no-nonsense manner that I wasn't a home run hitter and that I should hit the ball up the middle.

Just about the only team I didn't wear out that year was the Dodgers. I hit .271 against Los Angeles. There were two reasons for that. Number one, they always had a great pitching staff. And number two, Milton Berle would distract me. Uncle Miltie was a big baseball fan whom I met at Dodger Stadium. He would sit in his box seats next to the dugout eating sandwiches he'd brought from home. We developed a friendship. Whenever I'd bat at Dodger Stadium, Milton would call out my name, blow kisses, and sing, "I love you, Joey!" He used to invite me and some teammates over to his house for breakfast when we played in Los Angeles. Milton's been a great friend. He came to my fiftieth birthday party, and I went to his eightieth. He also was one of the many people who called me up looking for World Series tickets. He was in the stands when we won the Series in Game Six.

The 1971 Cardinals were the only team I ever played for that won 90 games. Still, we finished a distant second behind the Pirates. Even though we led the league in batting and stolen bases, we had little thunder in our lineup. While I hit 24 home runs and had a league-high 137 runs batted in, no one else hit more than 16 home runs or drove in more than 77 runs. I guess my MVP season also caused a lot more people to notice the success I had had with my water diet. All kinds of people, and not just baseball fans, were inspired by the fact that I had solved a lifelong weight problem and was able to keep the fat off. So many people wrote to the Cardinals and me that year asking how I did it, that the front office began mailing out copies of my diet. I must have been the only MVP in history who received more requests for a diet program than for an autograph.

I kept the weight off that winter, even though I was on the banquet circuit with my most valuable player award. Then I held out of training camp—again. It seemed like an annual event for me. But it did have a great benefit. I hated going to the start of spring training when all those young, wild-armed prospects would be trying to impress the coaching staff. In those days the hitting backgrounds were terrible in the Florida ballparks. It was dangerous, especially for a guy like me, who liked to crowd the plate. So I'd hold out until those young bucks were sent to the minor league camp. That year I wanted $150,000, a $35,000 raise after a MVP season. Bing Devine told me, "Anything under $150,000 is acceptable." That was the ceiling that Stan Musial and Bob Gibson had once established. I wound up signing a two-year contract worth $280,000.

I was hitting the ball great in spring training when Maxvill and I left for a players association meeting in Dallas with other player reps and alternate player reps. We were prepared to take a strike vote. Some of the players wanted to wait until the all-star break to strike. Marvin Miller told us, "At that time, four teams will be in first place. Are the players on those teams going to want to strike then? We have to be unanimous about this. If you want to strike, do it now or don't do it." Marvin painted a scenario that led us to believe it would not be a long strike. This wasn't about money, it was about benefits—the pension plan in particular. He said the owners were making too much money to let the strike go on. And so we voted to strike.

I returned to St. Petersburg with Maxie—I was his alternate—to tell our owner, Gussie Busch, that we were striking. That was horrible. Gussie was another owner who hated Marvin. We sat across

from him in a tiny office at Al Lang Field in St.
Pete. His son, August Busch III, was standing behind us near the door. Gussie pounded his fist on
the desk and roared, "Goddammit! That man is
leading you down a path to ruin! And he's getting
paid and you're not." I said, "Excuse me, but Mr.
Miller is not getting paid during the strike." That
pissed Gussie off even more.

Marvin was right—the strike didn't last long. It
was settled one week into the regular season. I was
in New York for the settlement—that was when
someone stole Frank's 1958 World Series ring out
of my hotel room. As part of the settlement, the
owners decided they were not going to make up the
games that were lost, even though it could easily
have been arranged with doubleheaders. Maxie
turned to me and said, "Did we win or lose this
thing?" The owners wanted to hurt us. They didn't
want to pay us. We all were docked about five percent of our salaries for the missed games.

Our club stood to lose more than most teams
with the settlement. That's because the Cardinals
had a history of treating their players better than
other clubs. For instance, they used to give everyone a single room on the road—that was unheard of
then. But after the strike was settled, the Cardinals
took away that perk and doubled up on rooms like
everyone else. It just so happened that they put
Maxie and me, the two union guys, in the same
room. We used to joke about sending someone else

up to our room to turn the key, thinking the room might be booby-trapped or something.

My union activity did not sit well with the fans. On opening day of the 1972 season, I was introduced in St. Louis for the first time as the most valuable player of the National League. They booed me. The decline of my career had officially begun.

CHAPTER 6
Three Outs

I WAS SITTING AT A BAR WITH BOB GIB-
son one night on the road with the Cardinals
early in the 1972 season. He was drinking
wine. I was drinking vodka. He could tell that I
was beating myself up inside about not hitting as
well as I had the previous year, when I won the
MVP award.

"Joe," he said, "I've got a question for you. Do
you really think of yourself as a .363 hitter?"

"Well, I . . ." I started to say.

"Tell me, what's your lifetime average?" Gibby
asked.

".305," I said.

"And what are you hitting now?"

".310."

"So what's your problem?"

Gibby knew me too well. We had become so

close over the last season that I couldn't hide anything from him. I was trying too hard to duplicate a once-in-a-lifetime season. It's difficult to be productive when you fight yourself like that, a problem I knew Tim McCarver experienced early in his career. I had other problems too. I couldn't relax because of my personal problems. I was trying to be a better husband and father to relieve my guilty conscience about the years of being too selfish about my career—and it just wasn't working out. My marriage to Dani was coming apart. She didn't like living in St. Louis very much, so we moved back to New York while I was playing for the Cardinals. That only made matters worse. The secret to playing baseball consistently well is to be relaxed enough so that you just react to things, as opposed to trying to force things to happen. I could no longer do that because I was too distracted and unhappy. I'd have a game here or there where I'd be able to get locked in and block everything else out, but for the most part I had too many negative thoughts creeping into my game. My numbers turned out to be decent but not up to the standards I expected. From 1972 through 1974 I batted between .282 and .289 for St. Louis without hitting more than 13 home runs or driving in more than 81 runs.

Ironically, as my career declined, I came as close to the World Series as I ever would as a player. In August 1973 we were in first place in the East Division, with a four-game lead. But then Gibson lan. "I couldn't have done it without him," I said. And then I said, "When I retire, I'm going to buy a shortstop. At night, when I'm lonely, I'm going to hit grounders to him."

From my days as a shy kid growing up in Brooklyn, the only thing I ever wanted to be was a ballplayer. I was happiest when I was on a ballfield, especially when it allowed me to escape problems at home with my dad or, later, with my marriages. But in 1975 for the first time in my life, I dreaded going to the ballpark. Baseball felt like work. I thought maybe it was time to quit. After the season, in which we actually finished two games over .500 in third place, Mets general manager Joe Mc-Donald said I could manage one of the Mets' minor league teams the next season. Even though my thoughts of managing had turned serious, I didn't want to retire on such a bad year.

I worked hard that winter at the Downtown Athletic Club in Manhattan with a trainer, Paul Mastropasqua, to strengthen the muscles in my shoulder and back. I also did a better job of accepting my part-time role, even if I still didn't like ... I hit the ball very well that year, finishing at 306. In August McDonald came up to me and said, "How would you like to go to the Yankees? They ant you, and I can work out a trade."

I thought, Hell, yeah. The Yankees were in first ace and looked like they were headed to the World Series. One of my old teammates with the aves, Billy Martin, was the manager. It sounded

tore ligaments in his knee while running the bases against the Mets at Shea Stadium. He fell so suddenly that my mother, who never missed a game when I played in New York, said it looked like he'd been shot. Gibby was such a fierce competitor that he insisted on trying to pitch the next inning. He threw one pitch that didn't even reach home plate, then collapsed on the mound. He pitched only once the rest of the season. We finished in second place, one and a half games behind the Mets.

I don't blame losing that season on Bob's injury, and I don't bother wondering what might have happened if he hadn't been hurt. I've always been the kind of person to deal with reality, not conjecture—a trait that has served me well as a manager. With the Yankees, for instance, I never brooded about not having my ace pitcher, David Cone, for three months. First of all, I was very concerned about his personal health after doctors discovered an aneurysm in his right shoulder. And secondly, there's nothing you can do about it once somebody goes down with an injury. Whatever players you have available make for the best team you could possibly have at that time. The worst thing you can do when someone gets hurt is to say, "If we had had that guy, we would have won this game." That has a negative effect on your team. That's why as a player or manager, I've never wasted time wishing for things that were not possible.

As painful as that 1973 season was, the next year was worse. I had been asleep in a hotel room in

Montreal on May 12, 1974, when the telephone rang at three o'clock in the morning. It's weird, but I knew exactly what it was about even before I picked up the phone: My mother was dead. She was sixty-nine years old and had died at a hospital on Long Island. Doctors listed the cause of death only as "heart failure," and we never ordered an autopsy.

My mom's death brought our family closer together. I realized that I had not been talking with my family as much as I did in the past. I knew they weren't crazy about my marriage to Dani, so I had drifted away from them a little bit. My mother's death brought on heavy feelings of guilt for me.

Four months later it was in that same hotel in Montreal that our pennant hopes ended. On the last day of the season, we were rained out of a game against the Expos. The first-place Pirates, who had a one-game lead on us, were playing the Cubs. We checked out of our rooms and were sitting around the hotel lobby while one of our announcers made telephone calls to get updates on Pittsburgh's game. If the Cubs beat the Pirates, we would play Montreal the next day in a makeup game, and if we won that, we'd play a one-game playoff in Pittsburgh. The Cubs looked like they were on the verge of victory, but then Chicago catcher Steve Swisher dropped a third strike, helping the Pirates to a winning rally that clinched the division for them.

I felt terrible. It was dark and wet in Montreal. The bus we took to the airport was quiet and sad. I had one more reason to feel awful: I knew I wasn't

going to be back with the Cardinals. The brought up a young first baseman from the leagues named Keith Hernandez and made hi gible for the playoffs if we won the East. right—a few weeks later St. Louis traded me Mets for Ray Sadecki. I quickly forgot abou ting to the World Series. I was going to a whose season had just ended with ninety-one

That was a very fragile time for me. On being unhappy with my marriage, I hit roc tom in the big leagues with a losing team. make matters worse, I became a part-time p hated it, and it showed. I had the worst s my life in 1975 with the Mets, batting .2 only good that came out of that season wa eventually made me a better manager. I th because I was an MVP and because I strug part-time player, I can relate to anybod roster. That's probably my biggest asset a ager. I experienced a huge range of emo cluding humiliation, as a player.

On one especially humiliating night year, on July 25 in a 6–2 loss to the H tros, I tied a major league record by grou four double plays, all of them against p Forsch. In every case Felix Millan had p of my grounders with a base hit. I've alw be a standup guy with the media, and was no different. I figure eventually you have to face them, so why prolong t even tried a little dark humor. First I tore ligaments in his knee while running the bases against the Mets at Shea Stadium. He fell so suddenly that my mother, who never missed a game when I played in New York, said it looked like he'd been shot. Gibby was such a fierce competitor that he insisted on trying to pitch the next inning. He threw one pitch that didn't even reach home plate, then collapsed on the mound. He pitched only once the rest of the season. We finished in second place, one and a half games behind the Mets.

I don't blame losing that season on Bob's injury, and I don't bother wondering what might have happened if he hadn't been hurt. I've always been the kind of person to deal with reality, not conjecture—a trait that has served me well as a manager. With the Yankees, for instance, I never brooded about not having my ace pitcher, David Cone, for three months. First of all, I was very concerned about his personal health after doctors discovered an aneurysm in his right shoulder. And secondly, there's nothing you can do about it once somebody goes down with an injury. Whatever players you have available make for the best team you could possibly have at that time. The worst thing you can do when someone gets hurt is to say, "If we had had that guy, we would have won this game." That has a negative effect on your team. That's why as a player or manager, I've never wasted time wishing for things that were not possible.

As painful as that 1973 season was, the next year was worse. I had been asleep in a hotel room in

Montreal on May 12, 1974, when the telephone rang at three o'clock in the morning. It's weird, but I knew exactly what it was about even before I picked up the phone: My mother was dead. She was sixty-nine years old and had died at a hospital on Long Island. Doctors listed the cause of death only as "heart failure," and we never ordered an autopsy.

My mom's death brought our family closer together. I realized that I had not been talking with my family as much as I did in the past. I knew they weren't crazy about my marriage to Dani, so I had drifted away from them a little bit. My mother's death brought on heavy feelings of guilt for me.

Four months later it was in that same hotel in Montreal that our pennant hopes ended. On the last day of the season, we were rained out of a game against the Expos. The first-place Pirates, who had a one-game lead on us, were playing the Cubs. We checked out of our rooms and were sitting around the hotel lobby while one of our announcers made telephone calls to get updates on Pittsburgh's game. If the Cubs beat the Pirates, we would play Montreal the next day in a makeup game, and if we won that, we'd play a one-game playoff in Pittsburgh. The Cubs looked like they were on the verge of victory, but then Chicago catcher Steve Swisher dropped a third strike, helping the Pirates to a winning rally that clinched the division for them.

I felt terrible. It was dark and wet in Montreal. The bus we took to the airport was quiet and sad. I had one more reason to feel awful: I knew I wasn't going to be back with the Cardinals. They had brought up a young first baseman from the minor leagues named Keith Hernandez and made him eligible for the playoffs if we won the East. I was right—a few weeks later St. Louis traded me to the Mets for Ray Sadecki. I quickly forgot about getting to the World Series. I was going to a team whose season had just ended with ninety-one losses.

That was a very fragile time for me. On top of being unhappy with my marriage, I hit rock bottom in the big leagues with a losing team. And to make matters worse, I became a part-time player. I hated it, and it showed. I had the worst season of my life in 1975 with the Mets, batting .247. The only good that came out of that season was that it eventually made me a better manager. I think that, because I was an MVP and because I struggled as a part-time player, I can relate to anybody on my roster. That's probably my biggest asset as a manager. I experienced a huge range of emotions, including humiliation, as a player.

On one especially humiliating night that awful year, on July 25 in a 6–2 loss to the Houston Astros, I tied a major league record by grounding into four double plays, all of them against pitcher Ken Forsch. In every case Felix Millan had preceded one of my grounders with a base hit. I've always tried to be a standup guy with the media, and that night was no different. I figure eventually you're going to have to face them, so why prolong the agony? I even tried a little dark humor. First I thanked Millan. "I couldn't have done it without him," I said. And then I said, "When I retire, I'm going to buy a shortstop. At night, when I'm lonely, I'm going to hit grounders to him."

From my days as a shy kid growing up in Brooklyn, the only thing I ever wanted to be was a ballplayer. I was happiest when I was on a ballfield, especially when it allowed me to escape problems at home with my dad or, later, with my marriages. But in 1975 for the first time in my life, I dreaded going to the ballpark. Baseball felt like work. I thought maybe it was time to quit. After the season, in which we actually finished two games over .500 in third place, Mets general manager Joe McDonald said I could manage one of the Mets' minor league teams the next season. Even though my thoughts of managing had turned serious, I didn't want to retire on such a bad year.

I worked hard that winter at the Downtown Athletic Club in Manhattan with a trainer, Paul Mastropasqua, to strengthen the muscles in my shoulder and back. I also did a better job of accepting my part-time role, even if I still didn't like it. I hit the ball very well that year, finishing at .306. In August McDonald came up to me and said, "How would you like to go to the Yankees? They want you, and I can work out a trade."

I thought, Hell, yeah. The Yankees were in first place and looked like they were headed to the World Series. One of my old teammates with the Braves, Billy Martin, was the manager. It sounded